McGregor Says

Special Days

Make
Lasting Memories

McGregor Says

Special Days

Make
Lasting Memories

Jim McGregor

Crystal Lake Press

To my first Editor, Frank Bucholtz who asked me,
"Would you like to write some stories for the newspaper?"
Thanks for opening a new door for me, Frank.

An Introduction to McGregor Says

For many years I had the opportunity to talk to the public from the pages of a local newspaper in Langley, British Columbia, usually reporting on emergencies or disasters or bringing a message of awareness or prevention.

My dad would read these weekly reports, put the paper down and say: "It always reads 'McGregor says'. When is it going to tell me 'McGregor does'?"

Now I have been given the exciting opportunity to share some time with you each week, usually on a lighter, more upbeat note. I knew a minister who used to say that every man and woman has at least one good sermon in them. But I am not going to preach to you. My Grandfather was an auctioneer who passed on a gift for the gab, but I am not going to try to sell you anything. I believe that when someone is given a chance to speak or write that they should make the best of it, educate, entertain, enlighten.

I know some people will read what I say and disagree, others will give their approval, and some won't understand at all. I know that because I learned years ago that you meet three kinds of people. People that make things happen, people that watch things happen and people that say, "What the heck just happened!?" Now each of you has just classified all your friends, family and co-workers into one of those categories, I know you did! You can break it down even simpler if you like. The world is made up of two groups, people who get it and people who don't get it! Unfortunately some people think they belong in one group when they are actually in the other. They just don't get it.

Hopefully my stories will have something for all groups. Maybe some columns will end with a poem because every day of your life is poetry whether you realize it or not. I may treat some situations seriously but I won't always take people seriously because they are for the most part, very funny. Especially the ones who think they are serious!

Stories will come from years ago, when I worked in the farm fields of Langley pioneers or they may be generated from an interaction with a family new to Langley. Events occurring in Langley today might be tied to history or, historical events may be used to illustrate why something is going off the rails today.

Langley has always been very good to my family and me and I'm sure that's because we always put a lot into making the community work. All the experiences of coaching, volunteering, running a family business, firefighting and raising kids, fill a well that holds so many stories.

These stories have been written over a ten-year period and it is interesting to see some of the phrases, technology or references to events has changed over that period of time. The reader may notice some repetition of phrases or thoughts and that just means they are important to me, and a reflection of how I approach life or celebrate family.

I would be most pleased to come to your home and find a coffee cup ring next to my book, where you set your cup down to think about something I wrote. Or maybe, find a stain from the marmalade that fell off your toast while you were laughing at a terrible pun.

The book starts with some Christmas stories and follows the special times of the year, but you can read it in any order that takes your fancy.

I hope to see you enjoy the stories, because as the song says, "Without an audience, there ain't no show!" Besides, it's healthy to sit and take a break once in a while. At least, that's what McGregor says.

Waiting for the Christmas Spirit

A check outside on Saturday morning revealed a clear blue sky and touch of early frost. After a few dark, dreary days, the sunshine was welcome and inviting. It seemed a shame to stay inside so, after a hearty breakfast and a second cup of coffee, I got a sudden urge to put up my Christmas lights.

Usually I procrastinate until I have to endure cold rain running down my sleeves as I cling to the slippery aluminum ladder. Today I won't have to battle the rain and I am buoyed by the fact that last year I bought a plastic tote, coiled the string of lights in neatly and marked the lid, "Outside Lights" before tucking them away.

Unexpectedly, I found myself humming Christmas carols as I stepped outside into the crisp morning air. That is unusual as the Christmas spirit usually eludes me until I'm finished looking after everyone else.

Christmas spirit affects everyone in a different way. Some start the day after Halloween, others stay in Grinch mode right up until the wrapping paper starts coming off the presents Christmas morning. Others just slowly let

1

themselves get swept up in the lights the color and the music, and finally give in.

I dragged the bin out of the shed and started taking the lights out. Some bulbs were twisted around others and the wires were caught up in the little plastic thingies that hold them onto the eve's troughs. In thirty seconds I had a big tangled mess.

I spread them across the lawn and plugged them in to replace any burned out bulbs. I stepped back and heard a crunch as I crushed a bulb with my heel. With the grace of a ballet dancer I spin, lose my balance and step on another one.

Now, every guy that has faced this will unplug the lights and try to twist the broken bulb out before getting the needle nose pliers. Now I need a Band-Aid. As I walk up the stairs my fingers are cold and I am no longer humming Christmas carols.

I make another cup of coffee and cradle my throbbing fingers around the cup. Instantly I recall winter days on my paper route with cold hands on the handlebars or changing tires on a semi on the freeway in a snow storm. I remember now why I don't enjoy winter.

I look out the window at the string of lights, coiled on the lawn ready to strike again like some colorful, venomous serpent. The little voice inside tells me I have to finish the job. The little voice sounds a lot like my Dad.

The exterior illumination scene from the movie Christmas Vacation strikes a chord in every man's heart. When Clark Griswold's lights come on, it is man's triumph over technology and we all cheer.

After waiting for my circulation to return and the sun to come out from behind the trees, I get the lights on the house. I haven't turned them yet, I'll wait for the perfect day closer to Christmas, put on a Mel Torme Christmas CD, and with a hot chocolate and a piece of my Mom's short bread in hand, I'll have my own personal lighting ceremony.

Christmas Spirit is a lot like the flu. You can try to avoid it but once it gets a hold on you, you have to let it run its course. At least that's what McGregor says.

A Christmas Story

I sat at my donated desk in the building housing the temporary offices of the Christmas Bureau. Roger Whittaker sang Christmas tunes from the portable CD player and the whole place was decorated in the sights and sounds of the season. A plastic tree with imitation presents occupied one corner and across the room, there was a selection of toys for kids to play with.

This was a different atmosphere than the structured, shiny, controlled environment I was used to. But, the busyness of the clients coming and going, picking up toys, registering for hampers, gave the place an air of excitement. The donations of food, clothes and gifts coming in steadily from businesses and individuals kept everyone too busy to question our surroundings. The business end of the operation was running smoothly. The volunteers were efficient and courteous and treated each new applicant with patience and respect.

I hung up the phone and looked up just as a young girl sat down at the registration desk, a very young girl with a very small baby in her arms. She didn't want to be there, I could see that by the way she avoided eye contact with our volunteer at the desk, but she complied with all the requests. She found two pieces of ID, and a care card for the baby. There was just the two of them, she told us.

Each request was a chore, as she had to move the baby from one arm to the other to take items out of her purse. One of our angels had noticed her struggles too and asked if she could hold the baby while mom registered. The child was delicately offered up and equally gently received.

I wondered what her story was. We all have a story, we write most of it ourselves but sometimes others take the pen from our hand and add a chapter or two. For most of us, a writer could not conceive a plot that would come close to the story on the pages of our personal journals. I'm sure when this young lady began her first chapter, this visit to us today was not part of her original plot.

I'm sure she imagined her boyfriend on one knee with a glittering ring, then a big wedding. She probably imagined a tidy house with Christmas lights on the eves and a tree by the fireplace, packed with presents, a room full of healthy laughter while she prepared a feast for her family. But it hadn't turned out that way.

Once the process was complete, the young mom thanked everyone, smiled at the lady with the baby as she handed her the child back. She started to go then stopped and turned around and, almost apologetically, said, "Thank -you so much, we really need this."

I'm glad we had a room at our inn for her and the babe.

This wasn't a rented vacant building to her, I'm sure it must have looked like a castle, a place of safety and refuge. It meant Christmas morning and Christmas dinner. It is not always easy to ask for help, but I'm sure you all know someone who could use some. You should give them a call. At least that's what McGregor says.

A Letter to Santa

Dear Santa:

I was at the mall today, leaning on the wall weary from shopping. I was watching you with the seemingly endless line up of children waiting to ask you if you could make their Christmas wishes come true. I'm not sure if it really was you, you see we have a problem with faith down here, we always need some kind of proof before we believe in anything.

Anyway, a lady came by with a four-year-old boy; she was in a hurry. The little boy looked at the giant candy canes, the huge chair and of course, he could hear your well-known laugh. "Can I see Santa, Mom?" he cried out. "No son," she replied, "the line up is too long and that's not what Christmas is about anyway." They disappeared in the crowd, but her answer to him lingered there in the mall.

As I looked around I thought, "What could the little boy possibly have seen that would tell him what Christmas was supposed to be about." All I could see was your display and many other huge signs declaring, "XMAS SALE". It seems more and more retailers, educators, and politicians are trying not to offend a minority of customers, parents, and voters. Instead, they offend everyone else, but so few of us stand up and say anything.

I was puzzled and then I thought, maybe you can answer my question:

> If Christmas is for Jesus
> Why don't we see him here?
> Why can't we climb up on his knee
> So we can whisper in his ear?
> The questions that we have for him
> About what he wants from you and me,
> If we're to celebrate his birthday,
> Why is Santa all I see?

> If Christmas is for Jesus
> Why is it all so loud and bright?
> When all he had was just one star
> To light a silent night;
> When no one rushed or hurried
> Or worried just how much to spend,
> When I'm sure the only gift he'd give
> Is love for family and friend.

> If we send Xmas cards, not Christmas cards,
> Put up an Xmas light display
> Then all we've done is used a cross once more
> To hide his name away;
> If Christmas is for Jesus,

Then we'll never grow too old;
We can still believe forever
In the Greatest Story ever told;
If we want them to believe us
It starts with you and me,
Then we can have a Christmas picture
Of our child on Jesus' knee.

It's not Xmas or the Holiday Season, in Canada it's Christmas. At least that's what McGregor says.

A Christmas Shopping Experience

A major retailers' association recently sent their members the results of a survey they had conducted regarding the biggest turnoffs customers have during Christmas shopping. The top three negative comments were, gaudy over-decorated stores, overly perky or pushy sales staff, and loud Christmas music. I would agree and probably add a couple more of my favourites such as overcrowding and over pricing.

Some stores definitely over decorate. The colors of Christmas used to be red and green but somewhere along the way purple, gold, silver and yellow have somehow become part of the scheme. The staff seems to have had a competition to see which one could slap up the most garland, string the most lights or put up the most metal trees. After that, they make the big XMAS SALE sign and put it in the window.

All the businesses have to bring on extra staff at Christmas time. There are two types of temporary employees. First we have the kid that doesn't want to be there at all but their parents told them they had to get a job.

They never smile. They are angry that this stupid job not only pays minimum wage but they also have to wear the dopey Santa hat all day. If they accidently make eye contact with a customer they look like deer in the headlights and pray, "I hope they don't ask me a question, I might have to talk to them."

The second type is the perky one the survey talked about. She greets you with a high-pitched Smurf voice. "Hi! Welcome to our store. We have many specials on today, including two-for-one on all Christmas decorations. Her voice is like nails on a blackboard and when you walk around the end of the aisle she doesn't recognize you and goes into the whole spiel again.

Then it becomes a game of hide and seek. The customer tries to find someone to help them while trying to avoid the one with the high-pitched squeal.

The loud music is one I agree with. If it was a soft medley of Christmas carols in the background to set the mood, that would be fine but some of the grating arrangements are hardly recognizable as Christmas music. Nobody should have to shout at Christmas time.

But it does increase sales. For instance, maybe the wife says to husband, "We should get a set of new silver wear for Christmas."

Because ABBA is screaming about a long time ago in Bethlehem, he thinks she said, "We should get the kids new underwear for Christmas," and he replies, "Sounds like a good idea." Next thing he knows $800.00 is going on the Visa card.

I long for the days when a store put up a real tree and maybe some lights and a cassette played soft music somewhere in the back. The staff smiled and waved and hustled over if you beckoned them and maybe even offered to giftwrap your purchase.

If you met an old friend or neighbour in the store you could carry on a conversation and not be drowned out or bumped or jostled. When you left, the staff would say Merry Christmas without the fear of getting reprimanded and the store owner would shake your hand and say, "Thanks for shopping here."

Make your store a welcome place and you might see more customers. At least that's what McGregor says.

Recipe for a Safe Holiday

Everyone enjoys decorating the family home for the
Christmas season; this simple recipe will provide many
happy holiday hours.

Ingredients
1 Christmas tree
1 Fireplace (clean)
Many assorted lights
Heaps of common sense
Colorful Decorations
Extinguishers and smoke alarms

Select a fresh cut Christmas tree
With a safe and sturdy base;
Water freely right away,
Then daily, just in case.

Blend colorful decorations
With lights, not cracked or frayed,
Make sure they're checked by ULC,
And approved by CSA.

Mix the clean, screened fireplace
With dry, well - seasoned wood;
No trash, no wrapping paper,
That does the flue no good.

Prepare the candles carefully,
Hot wax and flames can burn;
Spread heaps of common sense around,
That's how little children learn.

To garnish off this Christmas scene,
Wrapped presents add the charm;
Give extinguishers to your favorite friends,
To those you love, give smoke alarms.

New Year's Resolutions

"Fast away the old year passes, hail to all you lads and lasses." Robbie Burns was right on, where did it go? What kind of a year was it for you, did you get everything done you had planned? Did you go to the places you were going to go? Did you do all the things you like to do? I'm sure we all had some positive outlooks at this time last year, and now is a good time to reflect on where we went and where we're going.

I was discussing New Year's resolutions with some others and we all had theories on why they are successful or why they don't last past January 15th. When we examined the positive resolutions we noted that they were very simple, uncomplicated, and had very little to do with achieving world peace or stopping global warming. While some had tried to stop smoking, stop drinking or lose weight they were unsuccessful because they hadn't planned on the lifestyle changes those decisions require.

For instance, one individual resolved to quit smoking and was doing fine until he went back to work. As he sat as his desk adjusting his nicotine patch and chomping on a celery stick, he watched his old smoking buddies as they headed outside for a smoke. He suddenly realized he would no longer know who was doing what to whom in the office or who was on the verge of getting canned. He would no longer be in the loop and worst of all, he knew they would be talking about him. The reality was that he was mentally unprepared to join the ranks of the majority and it was as painful a sell out as cutting off his long hair had been to get a full time job in the seventies.

Weight loss is always hard too. The first week the Mueslix cereal tastes great and the skim milk is all right. But if your attitude is not right, if you are not truly convinced you want those new clothes and new lifestyle, then by February it seems you are pouring water on into a bowl full of gravel. Rice cakes become wedges of Styrofoam and you really start to dislike your perky new friends at the gym.

Keeping your resolutions simple is the key. A few years back, a wise man told me if I wanted to have a successful year I had to resolve that every day I should Drink, Swear, Lie and Steal. Now some of you just said, "Hey I'm with you", but let me explain.

You have to drink in all of the knowledge that you can absorb, learn new things every day and teach when you get the opportunity. Swear to do the best job you can do, an honest day's work for an honest day's pay. Do the best for your family, your friends your neighbours. Lie down for a moment and think about how blessed you are to live in this country, this province this Langley community. Think of where you are, where you've been and where you're going. Steal some time for yourself each day, time alone to re-group, examine what went right what went wrong and say to yourself, "Hey, how's it going?"

Look after yourself, get your own house in order, be part of the solution, and next year will start to look pretty good. At least that's what McGregor says.

The New World

Just suppose that someone, somewhere, had this amazing computer that had the power to erase last year at midnight on December 31st and give us a clean blank sheet to start with on New Year's Day?

Suppose there was international/cosmic decree that from now on, January 1st. each year would signal a new start for us all. We would start from scratch every year and it would be up to us to make choices that would determine how we ended up on December 31st.

Just but inputting our name, highlighting 2016 and pushing the delete key, everything we did last year would be gone. All the things we said that we wished we hadn't would be forgotten. All the bad advice we gave or received would not have been acted on and any money we lost would be back in our account.

For instance, you would wake up on New Year's Day and be the perfect weight for your height. Your blood would be pumping through clear arteries and your joints would be lubricated and fluid. No one would need glasses or hearing aids, arch supports or pacemakers. We would all be perfect.

We could decide if we were going to have a bowl of granola with peach slices and go for a healthy walk or we could fill the frying pan with grease and watch football and soap operas. Each day we would decide if we were going to maintain our perfect body or let it go.

All debts would be wiped clear under this new plan. We would start off with a positive balance in our accounts and as we went along, the financial decisions we made would either build our accounts or start to weigh us down. Would we learn from last year's mistakes?

The world would have no famine or poverty. Countries would not have enemies and all wars would be over on New Year's Eve. Could the politicians maintain the peace and share with those in need or how long would it take before the squabbling began again?

We would start fresh with families and friends. Anything we had said or done in the past year would be forgiven or forgotten and all our relationships would be as if we were meeting people for the first time. We could not carry over resentments or anger and some little transgression from twenty years ago would be long forgotten. Jails would be empty and the courts would be quiet.

There would be no one to blame for our human condition and it would be up to each one of us to make positive decisions about our personal health, finance, or relationships. We would control our own destiny and we alone would determine the success or failure of our new year.

This plan is not really new at all it has been around for a long time, it just takes too much work for most of us. But let's give it a try this year. At least that's what McGregor says.

2009 – The End of A Decade

We are now into the last year of this decade, 2009 is here whether we are ready for it or not. What's in store for us this year? Certainly the Olympics are just around the corner and as the year progresses so will the hype. Bridges and highways and event centers will have one ribbon cutting after another, the Olympic torch relay will bring it's excitement through our community and November and December will be nothing but Olympic headlines in the news.

That's a good thing. We should be proud to be hosting the world even if it is costing a lot more than we thought, but then it's always that way when we invite company to stay for a couple of weeks. We worry about how to pay for it when they've gone home.

It's certainly nothing compared to the last year of the previous decade, 1999. We focused on the world coming to an end at the stroke of midnight 2000, crippled by the Millennium Bug. Yes, all our computers were going to crash, telecommunications systems would fail worldwide and utilities around the globe would cease to function.

New words and phrases crept into our vocabulary. Y2K became a household world. It was an acronym developed by a computer programmer combining Y for year, Kilo, the Greek word for 1000 and 2 for 2000, henceY2K. I can only imagine the meeting that took place to come with that!

In Municipal government back then, Y2K was all about meetings. We developed local plans, Regional plans, Provincial plans and Federal plans. We produced binders with communications plans, staffing plans, mutual aid plans, and equipment deployment plans.

We heard that all our Fire Department systems would fail on the "Event Horizon", midnight on January 1st. 2000.

We bought back reports to council filled with complicated jargon explaining in depth why we needed to purchase expensive Y2K refit and software back up packages. However, after detailed, eloquent power point presentations, someone would ask, "What is Vancouver doing?" and we would end up doing whatever Vancouver was doing.

On January 1st. 2000 at midnight, with everyone on standby, nothing happened. In fact it was the quietest New Year's Eve on record. We went through our systems self-checks as per the manuals and it all worked.

Two opinions came out of all of that. One theory said nothing happened because the right preparations had been made in time. The Wall Street Journal reported Y2K was the 'hoax of the century' and cited countries that had done absolutely nothing, spent no money on Y2K and had the same results.

But in the aftermath, the contingencies put in place became valuable. New York put their Y2K plans into affect after 9-11 and the airline industry used their plans to ground all the aircraft. Locally, flood plans and mutual aid plans, all using those response guidelines have proven valuable over the years.

This year the press is going to be warning us of a recession. Do we get scared or do we just make sensible plans that that will hold true in good times as well? Practice moderation in our spending, eat well, stay healthy, look after our family first and do the right things for the right reasons, write a successful finish to the decade. After all, the reward for leading a good life is a good life, what more do you need? At least that's what McGregor says.

A Futuristic New Year

The New Year's bells will ring, the Time Square ball will descend, fireworks will explode, pots and pans will clatter in the midnight air and it will be 2011. To me, 2011 has a distinct science fiction ring. Many books and movies I read or watched years ago seemed to have amazing things happening in the 21st. Century.

Television shows like Twilight Zone or Outer Limits often had plots that took us into the next century where time travel or interplanetary flights were commonplace. 2001, A Space Odyssey was a classic movie that showed us all what to expect in the turn of the millennium and maybe the automation and robotics they depicted in that fictional story were not so farfetched after all.

Flash Gordon in the 25th Century, was a 1987 movie based on the 1930s comic book hero. In the movie and TV series, Flash had blasted off from a NASA base in 1987 and his mission went awry, keeping him frozen for 500 years. When he thawed out he tried to bring the 20th Century values into the new world. At the time it seemed like science fiction until all of a sudden in 2010 Bill Van der Zalm thaws out and shows up in the 21st. century. I'm sure it won't be long until he tries once again to give out shovels to the unemployed. B.C. politics is eerily like science fiction.

We have reached other planets with unmanned probes. Most of them seem to fail shortly after landing and provide us with only a smattering of data. I have no doubt that those failures are not by accident. I believe life on those planets is very much aware of us, maybe they have even seen some of our TV shows like Mork and Mindy, Lost in Space, or Third Planet from the Sun. If they have they will rush to disable our probes as soon as they land. After all, if you have had a quiet lifestyle for many centuries, would you want beings like us landing and populating there?

We were all fascinated by the futuristic means of communication in the future. Whether it was something simple like Dick Tracy's wrist radio or Mr. Spock's mind melding, they all seemed much more sophisticated than the big black phones we had stuck on our walls.

I did note that the Star Trek communicators always failed to work when the crew beamed down to the planet and never once did the Captain recommend changing providers. "Mr. Scott, cancel that TELUS plan and set us up with Shaw before the Klingons blow us out of the sky." Another question I had, if they could beam down to the planet, why did they have to walk to the transporter room?

As far as mind melding or communicating without speech or visual contact, that prediction has come true. It is commonly referred to as texting. This form of communication allows couples, friends or entire families to exist in communities or even homes without ever actually speaking to each other. This can only lead to the eventuality of humans losing the ability to speak at all. Not always a bad thing for some people I know.

A recent article listed the electronic devices that will be obsolete at the end of 2011; I have none of them. Happy New Year 2011, I'm not scared of you, bring it on. At least that's what McGregor says.

Optimism For the New Year

At the end of a meeting last month, the Chairperson was trying to set a date for a meeting in the New Year. She asked everyone to check their calendars and see if a bunch of busy people could come up with a date that worked for everyone.

As I was putting my papers away I noticed everyone was checking their phones, tablets or other devices and sounding out prospective devices. She was looking at me and I said, "I'll check my calendar and get back to you."

She looked a bit confused so I explained that "my calendar" was an actual calendar with a different classic car photo for each month and it was hanging in my kitchen. It has big squares for each day so that I can write in appointments and it works very well.

Each morning, as the coffee is pouring into the pot, I walk over and look at the calendar and it tells me where I am supposed to be, where at and what time. I'll admit, sometimes I struggle to read the scrawl that was hastily written while talking on the phone and on one occasion, I had written 'Friday the 18th' on the space for Friday the 18th

so I had to wait until somebody called me and asked if I was coming to the meeting that day.

It's not a perfect system but it works for me, and some weekends if there nothing written there, I'm not sure if I actually have the weekend off or if I've forgotten something. I was discussing planning ahead with a friend the other day and he explained that he doesn't share his plans for the day or the week with anyone. His explanation is that if you do too much planning, the word "premeditation" starts getting thrown around in the courtroom. He's not a close friend.

As my 2017 calendar is getting ready to be put up, this one with a different photo of a cabin on a lake, I have noticed that there are already a few days booked in January and even some into March, May and June and a couple as far away as September.

How optimistic we are that we plan that far ahead into our lives. Some say if you want to make God laugh, tell him your plans for tomorrow. Someone runs a red light, a piece of plaque lets go from an artery wall, one of your adult children shows up back at your door with their suitcases. Anyone of those events can wipe your calendar clean in an instant.

But it is the optimism and hopefulness that carries us forward. We should be looking forward to the March birth, the June vacation, and the September wedding. If we sit in the dark and expect the worst, that's probably what we'll get.

Wouldn't it be nice if we could treat the end of every day the way we treat December 31st? Imagine if we celebrated that we hand survived each day with banging pots wearing colored hats and were looking forward to the day ahead?

A card verse I received says, "Thanks for lessons, 2016! Plan each day to the fullest; make it worthwhile. It's not the years in your life that count, it's the life in your years. May the New Year be kind to you all. At least that's what McGregor says.

Bring on the New Year

It's a bit difficult to watch the national and International news when you live in Langley. Right now as I write this, the sun is peeking between the clouds and we sit at a balmy 12 degrees C. I have had a restful relaxing week with family and friends and ate way too much.

I know if I turn on the news I will see stories about the aftermath of ice storms or flooding back East and people who spent Christmas in the dark or maybe even a shelter because they lost their homes. I spoke to a man from Sudan recently who hasn't heard from his family since 500 civilians were killed in their village last week.

Once again we are entering the New Year in calm, peace and serenity in Langley. Even the two Langley Councils are talking to each other. We are pretty darn fortunate people.

I recently watched a documentary about 1914, one hundred years ago. The year started off reasonably well, many milestones were achieved. Henry Ford started his first Model T assembly line and raised employee wages to $5.00 a day, setting a new standard across North America. The

Panama Canal opened and changed maritime travel and commerce considerably.

The average person in North America was paying little attention to happenings along the Russia Austria border or the warnings coming from Germany. The political happenings there didn't really affect them. But by August the world was watching the beginnings of a terrible conflict that indeed would eventually be news in every City and Village around the world.

So how do we start our New Year on a positive note? Do we turn off the TV, do we cancel our subscription to the newspapers, and do we pretend the world doesn't exist outside the borders of Langley? Do we need to know about people losing their lives in Langley fires or why Langley RCMP are shooting at robbery suspects on 200th Street in the middle of the day? Those are sad and scary events in our peaceful little setting here.

Yes, we do have to know what is going on around us otherwise we begin to take things for granted and start complaining about nonsense stuff. We have to hope that other communities will see what we have and we hope we can set a standard.

This past summer as I worked with the Special Olympics Summer Games, I heard people from around the province rave time and again about our community, the people, the amenities, our facilities and I heard stories about people having to drive 40 miles to practice in their home towns. We hear Christmas Bureaus from other communities ask us how we get such amazing community support each year. We always reply that it is a very caring, giving community.

We have a choice. We can fill a bag of last year's troubles and worries and drag it along behind as we back into the new year or we can dust of our hands, hold up our heads and stride into the new year saying, 'Here we are, bring it on, we're ready for anything!'

A healthy, happy community is made up of healthy happy people. If you need any kind of help, you will find it here, all you have to do is ask. If you live in Langley, you are one of the luckiest people on earth. At least that's what McGregor says.

Looking Back, Looking Ahead

I'm too laid back this week to write a column so why don't you just grab a coffee or a cup of tea and we'll chat for a bit. Actually, I haven't done a thing all week except watch hockey and football, visit a bit, or pick at the turkey carcass. That's a good thing I think, to just take some time at the end of the year and take stock of where you've been or where you're going.

It's healthy to sleep in, walk around in your housecoat all morning, don't shave or answer the phone. Mind you after two or three days it's maybe not so healthy but the body and the mind need some down time. It's sort of like servicing your car, you can check it out once in a while and fix things or you can wait until it needs to be towed away.

So how was your year? Did you accomplish what you set out to? Did you look after those health issues or patch things up with relatives? Did you quit some thing bad or start something good? Did you get away or renovate, spend or save? Or was it just another year that passed at the speed of light leaving our good intentions somewhere along the way.

Better yet, how was your past decade? We are now into a new one and I suppose a change of decades should be some sort of milestone in our lives. We didn't start the last one so well with the World Trade Center disaster and the subsequent war. We all remember where we watched that life-changing event. Did you know the First Responders in the lobbies of those towers knew less about what was happening than we did watching CNN in our living rooms three thousand miles away? Did it change anything? Here we are the last week of the decade and the air travel security is again at its highest level since that week.

At the start of this decade most of didn't know where Kabul, Basra or Kandahar were but now they are household words. I'll bet when 1950 rolled around everyone was glad to see those terrible war years of the forties behind him or her. They were probably optimistic that all fighting and war would be over. Maybe this decade will be better; maybe we'll all learn to get along.

The first quarter of this year will be all about the Olympics and that will be exciting. My niece was named to the Canadian Women's Olympic Biathlon team last week so she'll be competing there. Do you remember where you were on that July day in 2003 when they announced "The 2010 winter Olympics are awarded to the City of Vancouver?" Yes almost seven years ago and there was so much to be done, so much controversy on the horizon but here it is. I seem to recall a major outcry about the negative effect Expo 86 was going to have but look at the positives that came from that.

So here we go into the unknown with lots of challenges ahead. I wonder if they'll make it better or worse during this decade. Will they learn from their past mistakes and who are "they"? The scary part is, what if "they" are "us"? Maybe we are the people that have to work to make it all better this time. At least that's what McGregor says.

Old Time Hockey On New Year's Day

On New Year's Day, over one hundred thousand people braved freezing temperatures in Detroit to attend the University of Michigan to watch the Winter Classic hockey game between Detroit and Toronto.

There is not normally a hockey rink on the field at the university but millions of dollars were spent to make millions of dollars so fans could come and watch a hockey game outdoors. Not exactly like the old timer with a hose who comes out to flood the local rink but it seems to have attracted a lot of interest.

During the game the announcers kept repeating the phrase, "just like old time hockey from days gone by." I wish my Dad could have been sitting on the couch beside me watching this game. I could hear his running narrative arguing with everything the commentators were saying.

We have a couple of old black and white team photos of my Dad's hockey team from Edam Saskatchewan. They are a tough looking group of unsmiling prairie farm boys, and according to Dad, they were feared wherever they went.

So when the commentators talk about the hand warmers the players have inside their gloves, I would have heard about the one pair of gloves Dad had to last an entire season and by the last few games there were holes in the fingers and the palms.

When they showed the propane heaters at the player's benches I would have heard the story about how the opposing team didn't clear the snow or ice from the visitors' benches and if you sat down you froze to the wood. There was no warm air to comfort the players when they came off the ice.

When they showed the "retro pads" the goalies were wearing I recalled how one day I told Dad I needed shin pads for soccer. I heard the story about when he played hockey no one could afford shin pads so they had catalogues or newspapers stuffed inside their socks held in place with skate laces or binder twine.

The old pictures show very little padding and no helmets or cages. A lady comedian observed once that male hockey players started wearing jock straps almost a hundred years before they started wearing helmets. It's all about priorities when it comes to protection.

If a player did get injured in the Winter Classic, the trainer and the team doctor whisked them away to the warm confines of the dressing room. Dad would tell stories about players continuing to play with broken bones or cuts because there weren't enough players to allow someone to sit out. A band-aid or cigarette paper would be put over a cut or, if bad enough, the coach or another player would stitch it up with a needle and thread.

When the commentator talked about the team busses having problems getting through the snow and the traffic, Dad would have scoffed and regaled me with the stories about five or six guys jammed into a car travelling miles across frozen grid roads. If the wheels bounced out of the ruts, the players would get out and lift the car back in place.

But I guess if you have million dollar players it's a good idea to keep your investment warm and comfortable. After all, we wouldn't want them to go on strike. I think that Edam team could have beaten the Maple Leafs. At least that's what McGregor says.

Time to Start Fresh

We were sitting around the coffee shop discussing how we had spent New Year's Eve and I must say that the fact everyone in my group remembered what they did New Year's Eve was pretty boring. I seem to recall that in the past, New Year's Day was a combination of water, Alka-Seltzer and apologies. It's not a bad thing that all of that is behind us. Well, most of us.

Some stayed at home, some went to a house party or New Year's function. Some were designated drivers or took taxis. When the stories don't involve interactions with Police, Firefighters or tow truck drivers they are actually pretty lame.

One of the group said, "It's just another day, a flip of the calendar page. The days fall one after the other and there really is no start or end to the year." What an interesting point of view. Personally, I disagree, my life has to have a start and finish to the year otherwise nothing would get cleaned or organized.

Just starting a new folder titled January 2015 gives me a feeling of accomplishment and anticipation, ready to go, let's get things done this year.

I would like to go one step further and have a big "DELETE" button installed in each home. Wouldn't it be great at one minute after midnight to push that big do over button and have everything from last year disappear?

There would be no bills to carry over, we would start financially fresh and promise to handle our spending and buying much better this New Year. Imagine if all the stupid things we had said or done during the past year just vanished and the people we had wronged or upset would forget about it and their resentments against us were forgotten?

With a push of the button any health related issues from last year are gone. We start with healthy lungs, great blood pressure and lots of lubrication in all our joints. There would be no medications lining our windowsills or filling our medicine cabinets. We would go back to that part of our life where we could eat or do anything we wanted to do.

But being human, would we abuse this arrangement knowing full well that no matter what we did during the year we could push the big button in January and start all over? Or would we learn from our mistakes. Would we eat healthier, would we exercise more, would we invest and save our money, would we be more compassionate and caring to those who mean the most to us?

I'm sure many of you have seen the analogy of each day being a bank of 86,400 seconds and every morning that amount of time is deposited in our personal "bank," There are no restrictions, we can spend those seconds any way we want but they are gone at midnight.

How much have you got from those seconds of time you were given today? Did you waste some? Spend them frivolously? Did you start something new, or finish a project? Did you meet someone new or make contact with an old acquaintance, lest they be forgotten?

The analogy suggests that if those second were dollars we received every day, knowing we couldn't carry them over, we would likely pay much more attention as to how we spent them.

You won't get them back. Invest your time wisely. At least that's what McGregor says.

Don't Forget Your Valentine

Valentine's Day is right around the corner. I know that because twice this week I have heard Leapy Lee singing "Little arrows in your clothing, little arrows in your hair." Now you too can hum that tune for the rest of the day.

I checked with my grandson and they are still observing Valentines at his play school, which means that some obscure religion has not convinced a newly created Ministry to outlaw it.

It can be a stressful time for some. Remember cutting out a Valentine for her and putting it the little envelope, wondering if she would give one to you? It is a delicate time. Let me tell you about two friends.

Friend number one was called out of town to work and was away for Valentines Day. He is by nature a thoughtful person, but he was very busy. He neglected to call, send a card or flowers. He returned home to find new furniture in his house. "A Valentine's present", she said. Note to file, flower delivery trucks are much smaller and less expensive than furniture delivery trucks, even on Valentine's Day.

Friend number two is very organized and methodical; he got married on Valentine's Day. What a great call. Now, every card manufacturer, chocolate producer and diamond merchant starts reminding him of his anniversary two days after New Years and, he has eliminated one present and one dinner by combining two occasions. That reduces relationship stress immensely.

The day takes some planning. Yes, roses are expensive but so are sofas and kitchen cabinets. For all of us—male or female—just the little bit of extra attention is nice. For instance, going out for dinner is good and a movie or play after is better. However going out for dinner and saying, "Let's get home in time to watch the Canucks/Minnesota game," may lower your scoring to the Markus Naslund level.

As a public service, I have included a poem today that you can cut out or copy and paste into a Valentine card for your significant other. The message is quite simple. If you treat every day as Valentine's Day, then no extra planning is required, at least, that's what McGregor says.

Every Day Is Valentine's With You

I'll send you roses on a summer day,
Cinnamon hearts the first of May;
In June, a rhyme that violets are blue;
I'll send you chocolates in December,
So each new month you'll remember
That every day is Valentine's with you.

The clouds up high in the August sky
All look like hearts to me;
Every morning on my pillow
Cupid's arrow's all I see.
There's so much love to go around,
One single day won't do;
My calendar says every day
Is Valentine's with you.

With snowflakes falling all around,
When autumn leaves are tumbling down,
I'll call every day to say my love is true;
With the first new day each spring
I'll teach the early birds to sing
That every day is Valentines with you.

Those cards arriving in your mailbox,
Each one of them is mine;
Every day they've come to say,
Please be my Valentine.

Go the Extra Mile

Valentine's Day falls on a Saturday this year. That makes it a bit more of a challenge for the men. When that day for lovers is during the week, there are many more opportunities for excuses as to why they didn't pay as much attention as they should have.

After all you had to get up and go to work. It was too busy during the day and you didn't get a chance to get out for lunch. Traffic was bad on the way home and you didn't want to stop for gifts and cards and be late. Guys can be quite creative when they are trying to save their own skin.

But Saturday, they are trapped at home and there is plenty of interaction with his significant other so it can be tense if he hasn't thought ahead. For instance, when he sits down for his morning coffee, if there is a red envelope resting against his cup and he doesn't have the trump card in his housecoat to return, it starts to get dicey.

Worse yet, if he has missed some signals during the week, he is now playing from behind. For example, if at some time on Tuesday or Wednesday his wife casually mentioned, "I have a sitter for Saturday night," and the only significance to his Saturday night is that the Canucks are playing the Flames on Hockey Night in Canada, he is heading for the rapids and the waterfall is in sight.

So then, many young men think they can salvage the day. They make a trip downtown to buy cards, flowers and chocolates and after racking their brains to remember what her favorite restaurant is, they optimistically phone for a reservation.

Now the mature husbands know that trying to make a dinner reservation on Valentine's Day is a fool's game, especially on a Saturday.

The young guy then compounds the error by pretending he has reservations somewhere and after walking into the third restaurant and being told there is a ninety-minute wait, the dew has dried on the grocery store roses. Worse yet if they end up at a pub and he takes the seat with a view of the Canucks game on the big screen, the evening is all but over.

I read an article that reported the results of a survey that says that a high percentage of men observe Valentine's Day only as an obligation or as a chance to get lucky. The term "getting lucky" changes as you get older. An old-timer friend of mine says his definition of getting lucky is finding a woman who can still drive after dark.

But surely there must still be some romantic guys out there. A simple blank card that that says I love you with a handwritten note inside recalling the first time you told her you loved her is priceless. Follow that up with a reservation to a new place you made weeks ago and then putting on a tie and sports jacket to take her to dinner. She just wants to be set apart from all the other women who received the rubber stamped cards and heart shaped boxes of chocolates.

One last tip for you young guys, if she has told you she doesn't want anything for Valentine's Day, don't believe her for a second, it's a test, and doing nothing is not an option. At least that's what McGregor says.

Selecting the Right Valentine

The little girl and boy in front of me at the checkout counter were clutching packages of Valentine cards. I had to wonder if the same events would be taking place this week in their classrooms that we had at Langley Central School many, many years ago.

At some point during art class, before Valentine's Day, we would make some sort of large envelope to capture all our expected cards. The project began with cutting pasting and folding construction paper then decorating the outside with hearts or some sort of designs.

The finished envelope would either hang from our desk or maybe the class would put them all up along the wall together. The most important feature was to display our names in big print making it easy for the others to find.

One night at home, we would spread the valentines out on the kitchen table. With scissors and glue and a sharp pencil at hand we would begin the task of selecting the proper card for the right classmate.

The teacher was the easiest. There was always a card that said something clever like 'To my Teacher ' so that was an easy one. You made sure to print your name in big letters as there was always the urban legend that if your teacher didn't get a Valentine from you, you might not pass that year. No sense taking any chances.

You had to be careful when selecting the cards. Some might have the right picture for a certain classmate but the wording would be wrong and you didn't want to send a wrong message to a girl or get thumped by a boy. But after some sorting, it began to work out. First the guys: Bob, Terry, Glenn, Gary, Joe, David, and Richard. Then the girls: Cynthia, Susan, Gail, Grace, Rebecca, Linda, or Joan. All of them pretty easy names to spell.

But then came the most delicate situation of this task. Picking out the Valentine for "Her." A crush on a girl in grade four is a very serious thing indeed. You can't let any of your male friends know you like this girl because they will ridicule you mercilessly and worse yet, maybe tell her. You certainly can't tell her because what if she doesn't feel the same way about you. Then you would have to ask your parents to move to another town.

So you fuss over the picture. You don't want her thinking you are making fun of her. You stress over the verse. It can't be too personal to give you away but it should say more than you said to the other girls.

Once the decision is made, then comes the printing of Her name. It must be letter perfect and you write it as if you are engraving on the crown jewels. Surely she will notice the difference in your writing from the clumsy scrawl of the other boys.

On the big day, you carefully open your envelope to see if she left one for you. You read the message, look at the picture and the writing to see if she has left a clue for you. After you are pretty sure she did, you keep Her Valentine separate from the rest.

Take some time, send a special message to your Valentine this year. Pretend she's the girl who sits three rows over and two seats down. At Least that's what McGregor says.

The Cost of Love

My friend was working in a flower shop one Valentine's day. That's the equivalent of working in a tire shop on the first day of snow, everybody wants it now and the price is not negotiable.

A customer had waited in line and plunked down a fancy Valentine card. She rang it up and said, "That will be $6.35 please." He looked at her in shock and replied, "For a card, I don't think so!" and walked out. When she went to put it away she noticed it read: "To my wife who means everything to me". Well everything up to $6.35.

Everyone who has ever had kids or grandkids has a kindergarten construction paper Valentine tucked away somewhere. Its value is priceless; you can't buy love. It is a slippery slope when you try to apply a value to love, and men are very disappointed that there is no Valentine's equivalent of Boxing Day when roses return to being just flowers.

But February is not a romantic month. Rain, snow, and storms are usually not your classic romantic settings, so candy and flowers become the standard. If Valentine's Day

was in July you could steal her away for a romantic picnic
lunch:

A special friend, a picnic basket,
With chilled red wine and gourmet cheese;
A secluded spot, where the only sound,
Is a whispered promise
On a summer breeze.

But then again, if you're truly in love, a snowstorm can
be romantic and inspiring:

If each snow flake that I'm watching
Held a memory or two
Of every time we've kissed each other
I'd be knee deep in love with you.

If each snow flake that I'm catching
Was a time I'd held you tight,
I soon would have my hands full
And it would have to snow all night.

If each snow flake that I'm counting
Marks each minute we've spent apart,
Then I soon will need some sunshine
To melt the drifts around my heart.

Yes, true relationships are built to survive storms,
tragedies and the spiraling cost of roses:

The wind blown leaves and the driving rain,
Bounced wildly off the windowpane;
Inside was warm and quiet instead,
As two lovers snuggled close in bed.
To them the gale did not exist,
It disappeared with every kiss;
For lovers, skies are always clear,
And storms are something love can't hear.

I think the only thing better than receiving expensive roses on Valentine's Day, is getting roses any other day of the year for no reason at all. At least, that's what McGregor Says.

Valentine Primer

Valentine's Day is less than a week away. I usually try to give men a few tips on how to survive this very important occasion. One slip up can be very costly.

First, when purchasing the Valentine's card actually read the verse and be sure it applies to your relationship. Do not buy one based on price alone. Often, men make the mistake of buying a humorous Valentine card, which can be dangerous. Believe it or not, some things men find hilarious are not funny to women at all.

Maybe you have decided to buy chocolates. Do not buy the boxes of chocolates next to the grocery store checkout. Your lady has seen them and knows they are cheap and on sale. You have to go to a specialty chocolate store, in a mall or in some trendy little village. The chocolates aren't that different but the box and bag will have the store name on them and this shows you put some thought into it. When the clerk rings them up and says, "That will be $25.70, please," you must resist the urge to blurt out, "You're kidding, for a box of chocolates!?" It is all about sentiment and romance is expensive.

Flowers are a nice touch and you can't go wrong with roses. You may be tempted to go with a big colourful arrangement, but admit it men, no matter how long you have known this woman you have no idea what she is allergic to and you don't want her clogged up and sneezing for three days. Those will be long days for you. Also, pay the extra and have them delivered; she will like it when the neighbours see that.

Lingerie can be a very tricky purchase. Many men are drawn to the trashy Playboy bunny items but you are wise to go with the more elegant Victoria Secret fashions. You are sending a message here and you don't have Hugh Hefner's money.

When it comes to size and you are trying to decide between 8-10 or 10-12, choose the 6-8 and get a gift return receipt. It is much safer to say, "Wow, I was sure you were no bigger than a six," rather than, "Holy cow, I thought 12 would be plenty big enough. "

Dinner and a movie is a great idea but for Pete's sake guys, make a reservation. Too many men assume that they are the only ones who thought about taking their lady out on Valentine's Day. If you can walk in and say, "Smith for two at six o'clock," and be whisked away to your table, all the other wives jammed into the restaurant foyer will be giving their spouses the glare. You know the one.

When choosing the movie find the one advertised as "Mother reconciles with estranged daughter who has leukemia, a love story for the ages." Resist buying tickets for the one with "Thrill a minute action and car chases". This could result in a very quiet ride home.

Let's recap: card presented in bed, chocolates and lingerie placed on the dining room table with a note about the dinner reservations, roses delivered about an hour before you come home, hold her hand in the movie when she starts to cry, tell her you love her.

Remember, this one day can set the stage for the rest of the year. At least that's what McGregor says.

Valentine's Day Memories

Valentines Day brings promise to all ages; this is a weekend for lovers. I enjoy hearing stories how couples met, where they were what made that meeting so special. Sometimes it can be a glance across a crowded room, love at first sight. It is inspiring to think that two souls could lock together in an instant and they try not to think what may have happened if one had been looking the other way. Here is some of my poetry for lovers.

Just a Glance

I glanced across the crowded room
And saw her sitting there;
Dark smoldering eyes, a magic smile
And long, black velvet hair.

Her gaze met mine, one eyebrow raised
And much to my surprise;
I was struggling for answers
To the questions from her eyes.

Should I start a conversation?
Should I ask her out to dance?
Should I tell her what she's done to me
With just a single glance?

What excitement lay before us,
So much danger hides within;
But I know that to avoid an end
We just should not begin.

As quickly as our thoughts had touched
We turned our heads away;
Our hearts were hiding promises
Our eyes should not betray.

Now that night is just a memory
That we share each Valentines,
So thankful that our hearts won out,
When her glance embraced with mine.

Do you remember a fragrance, an aftershave, a pipe tobacco? Of course you do, it came to you the minute you read that. They say our olfactory memories can be the strongest and most lasting of any of our senses. But what if a perfume lives up to its name and becomes an obsession? What if you have to see her every time it caresses you, awake or asleep? That's probably love too.

Obsession

I wonder what kind of perfume she wears,
I'd like to buy a small bottle to keep;
I'll sprinkle a few little drops on my pillow
So she'll be in my dreams when I sleep.

I'll spray just a little on my shoulder or sleeve
Then pretend she is standing right there;
Fantasize she is talking and laughing,
Casually brushing my cheek with her hair.

I'll take some to work, and, there in my office,
Just dab a small bit on my phone,
The rest of the day I'll put people on hold,
And talk to her all alone.

That scent she wears is some Voodoo potion,
Designed to catch me unawares;
So instead of doing something productive,
I'm a slave to the perfume she wears.

Don't waste the weekend, if your Valentine is with you; take some time to make some new magic. If all you have left of your Valentine are memories, then take some quiet time and close your eyes. Remember the glances, the smiles, the fragrances all the things you shared that will never leave. Love endures all; at least that's what McGregor says.

Say It with Poetry

This is my annual reminder to everyone, specifically men, Valentine's Day is approaching. Yes boys, each year on February 14th, many people exchange cards, candy, gifts or flowers with their special "valentine." The day of romance we call Valentine's Day is named for a Christian martyr and dates back to the 5th century, but has origins in the Roman holiday Lupercalia.

It's hard to believe that for over 16 centuries many men have forgotten to recognize this romantic date and have paid dearly for the rest of the year. A woman may tell you out loud that's it's "not a big deal," but don't believe that for a minute.

Usually something personal will fit the bill for a gift and, just the fact you've remembered and made the effort, will be well appreciated. Today, I'm going to mentor you to write a poem to your Valentine, then you just have to buy a blank card, write the poem inside and present it with a bottle of wine and a rose.

Don't tell me you can't write a poem because everyone has romance hidden inside and it just has to be channelled. Often by simply taking something you enjoy and equating to your significant other makes the task easy.

For instance if you are someone who likes working with wood in your shop, your poem could start, "I love your warm and tender touch, when I am in your hands; You turn me and you shape me, you're the one who understands." See how easy that was? You just took words from your hobby and made them about her.

For my car guy friends this could be a bit more difficult. For instance, my friend Clay, might write, "When I'm with you, it's just like heaven; when you're purring like a three twenty-seven." It rhymes nicely but you are writing romantic poetry and comparing her to an internal combustion engine could be risky.

Maybe you work in an office all day, let her know you are thinking about her, "When I spin in my chair and look at the view; no scenery in the world compares to you!" She will be thinking, "Golly, he's supposed to be working and he's sitting there thinking about me!"

Possibly you are a truck driver on the road all day and away from home a lot. You could put her right there in the cab with you by simply writing, "These roads I may drive alone but I am never lonely; you're here with me, you're all I see, you are my one and only."

Try to stay away from using names. Many names today can be hard to rhyme to and it makes your poem restrictive. Using terms like "Honey", "Sweetheart" or "Darling" is much better. For example, "When I think of you, Lorraine," automatically limits what the next rhyme is. But if you start, "Darling, when I think of you," you have much more to work with. Also, if you aren't with Lorraine next Valentine's day, you can re-use the generic poem on your new lady.

Yes boys, a sentiment from the heart, in your own hand writing will remind her of those little elementary school Valentine's Days when the boys printed their own names on those little paper valentines.

Make an effort. Be romantic. At the very least don't forget to say, "I love you." At least that's what McGregor says.

A Valentine Afternoon

"Take the afternoon off," he said as he finished his coffee.

"It's Monday," she replied.

"I know but it's Valentine's Day, let's do something."

"Like what?" she asked.

"I don't know, we'll think of something."

"OK, I'll meet you here at noon." She pecked him on the cheek and left the house.

He was home before her and propped the card he had bought against the bowl on the kitchen table. It was too cold to go for a walk on the beach. Maybe he could suggest a movie or just go somewhere for a long lunch. Now that he had made the suggestion, it seemed he couldn't think of anything she might like to do. Suddenly it felt like their first date all over again.

Right at noon she walked in, carrying some grocery bags.

"What's in the bags?"

"Just some snack stuff, I thought we'd just stay here for the afternoon." She laughed.

"At home, you just want to stay here and do nothing?" He questioned.

"Sure, who's going to look for us at home? Besides I think if we use our imagination, we can think of lots to do right here, like the old days."

He set the groceries on the counter, took her hand and spun her around as the radio played an old song. They danced across the kitchen, weaving around the chairs and out into the hallway, and the afternoon slipped away.

You can buy wine and roses, you can buy jewellery and chocolate, but you can't buy time. Sometimes, time is something you have to steal. At least that's what McGregor says.

Dance in the Kitchen

Out of the blue
I arrived home at noon
On a Monday when nothing was planned;
I heard you come in,
Smiled back at your grin,
Took the groceries from your hand.
We stopped and stared
There were sparks in the air
We could just hear the radio play,
So while Seeger was singing
"We've got tonight"
We danced in the kitchen today.

We danced in the kitchen
But it seemed like a ballroom,
We waltzed past the table and chairs.
We danced in the kitchen
With nobody watching,
Past the dog and the cat's worried stares.

That afternoon drifted away,
I whispered those words I never say;
Gliding and turning,
Smouldering then burning,
We danced in the kitchen today.

Jim McGregor

Come and dance close beside me
With my arms around you
Just come and dance me away,
Who needs tomorrow?
Who needs a dance floor.
If we can dance in the kitchen each day!

Easter Promises a New Start

The story goes that a small town was over run by squirrels. They infested the stores, the banks the restaurants; business was at a standstill; The Mayor noticed that the only place not affected was the local church so he approached the minister and asked how he kept the squirrels out. The minister replied, "I baptized them, made them members, now they only show up at Christmas and Easter."

Certainly, many people will be in the pews this weekend as Easter continues to be one of the most significant of all the religious observances. Many people embrace the literal Bible story of the rock being rolled away and the resurrection, the promise of life after death, a second chance.

Others tend to lean to the more commercial, chocolate worship of the Easter Bunny. A lot of families combine the two and add a family gathering, maybe a big dinner with relatives and friends. Personally, I like the symbolism of the rock rolling away and giving us a second chance, a new start. That is what spring affords us all and that rock can take on many forms.

We can imagine nature putting her shoulder to that terrible rock of winter and pushing it aside to allow the sun and warmth to resurrect the colors and beauty of spring, making us all feel alive again coaxing us from our drab, dark caves. Perhaps it's the time of year to set aside rocks and boulders in our back yards and parks and once again plant new seeds in our gardens and our communities.

Possibly, your rock may be an addiction or a bad habit that has been holding you back, blocking your path. What better time than spring to peer around the sharp, craggy edges of that barrier, to see the possibilities of a freer life ahead. Maybe just move it enough to reach out a hand and ask for help. It will roll away so much easier if other hands are there to help push.

The Easter story not only promises us rebirth but also illustrates the power of forgiveness. Who among us can easily ask for forgiveness for those who have pierced our hearts, or nailed us to our own private crosses? But what a great opportunity to roll away a huge rock of resentment that may exist between you and a friend or family member! It has been said that harboring resentments or ill will against someone is like taking a daily drink of poison yourself and waiting for the other person to die.

Many "squirrels" don't feel the need to attend church each week and lead exemplary Christian lives. Many regular church attendees are still lost and searching in the depths of their tombs. I believe it is important to find your own sanctuary, the spiritual places where you personally can communicate with the God you understand.

So, let's look forward to the new chance we've been given once again, the opportunity to get around the obstacles on our journey and move ahead. The new path may not always be the easy one, we may need renewed faith to traverse new rocky roads and solve new problems.

But remember, we were never promised a calm passage, just a safe harbor. At least, that's what McGregor says.

Having a Simple Easter

A picture on a website caught my eye this week. It was a photo of a large glass bowl filled with Easter eggs. It was the simplicity in the photo that attracted me. The eggs were blue, red, yellow, green and purple. They didn't have sophisticated designs on them; they weren't stenciled with graphics or messages. They were just colored eggs.

The only thing missing was the names, Ellen, Jack, Betty, Jim, Gord, Ken, Mom and Dad. Of course those were applied with a wax candle prior to dunking the eggs into the cups arranged in a row along the counter.

The cups were filled with hot water and vinegar and then a couple of drops of food coloring were added to each one, maybe more if you wanted a darker color. It was a pretty simple process until someone decided they wanted a multi-color egg. The production was carried out under the supervision of Mom or a big sister and the tricky part was taking them out with a big spoon and not dropping them or cracking the shell.

It's a pretty simple memory but just remembering all of us in the kitchen at the same time, laughing and making a mess is what our family home was about.

Easter Sunday meant grey slacks, white shirts, ties and blazers for the boys and dresses, and hats for the ladies. I recall a minister once saying he was so impressed with the Easter Sunday fashions that he went down from the pulpit and remarked to a six-year-old girl what a beautiful Easter dress she was wearing. She leaned into the microphone and sweetly replied, "Thank-you, but my Mom says it's a bitch to iron."

Easter Sunday also meant a longer sermon than usual. My brothers and I have permanent pinch marks on our shoulders administered by a big sister in an attempt to curtail fidgeting. The church was full and the pews were crowded and non-regulars often upset the apple cart by sitting in a regular member's permanent nest.

Everyone looked their best, we were all turning that corner into that new season we had been promised, the rock of winter was being rolled away and re-birth was all around us.

In the midst of the celebration, we may notice an emphasis on Easter goodies and chocolate bunnies. Though these traditions can make for a festive Holiday, it's important to take a step back to remember why we celebrate Easter, just as it's important to have a meaningful Thanksgiving or Christmas.

Contrary to what some children may believe today, the two Marys were not on an Easter egg hunt when they found the rock had been rolled away from the tomb. But complacency can easily blend stories together and eventually the truth gets lost.

The four-day weekend allows for travel time and provides a great opportunity for families to gather, eat too much, and share memories. Some insist that ham is the Easter meal and others go with a traditional turkey but either way, it doesn't have to have fancy a Martha Stewart touch, you can fill up on conversation.

Make sure you pick up some food coloring, vinegar and eggs when go shopping this week, have everyone color their own egg and see what happens. Remember, if you do go to church for the first time this year, make sure you're not sitting in someone's spot. At least that's what McGregor says.

Time to Be Born Again

Why isn't Easter on the same weekend each year? It seems that in western cultures, the Easter dates are based on a lunar calendar very similar to the Hebrew calendar and way back in 325 AD they started to set the Easter dates based on the first Ecclesiastical full moon after March 20th. Does that clear it up for you?

I wonder if anyone has told Mother Nature about this sophisticated arrangement. She is probably just as busy as any other mother and I'm sure she would be more than happy to have it set on the same weekend every year. After all, March and April are very tricky weather months and while she is popping up daffodils in Vancouver she is still dumping snow back east and moving the Easter days around each year is no doubt a very real source of irritation to her.

Nature's changes are constant and controlled by forces that do not have the constraints of calendars or clocks. We however, need to have some sense that we are in control. We move our clocks ahead and back to suit our needs or we add a day once every four years. But the tides come and go, the sun rises and sets and the moon waxes and wanes over us the same as it did for the cavemen.

We can imagine nature putting her shoulder to that terrible rock of winter and pushing it aside to allow the sun and warmth to resurrect the colors and beauty of spring, making us all feel alive again coaxing us from our drab, dark caves. Perhaps it's the time of year to set aside rocks and boulders in our back yards and parks and once again plant new seeds in our gardens and our communities.

The four-day Easter weekend is a welcome break. The fact that it comes later this spring will surely be a boon for the hardware and gardening stores as folks hope the skies will clear and the temperature warms up so we can finally can finally start working outside.

I need that warm sun to coax me outside. After all, when there is hockey, baseball, golf and curling on the TV all at once, you don't feel quite as guilty sitting inside channel surfing when it is pouring rain.

But the stores are all geared up for Easter with Chocolate and gifts. I noticed large chocolate bunnies, a chocolate Spiderman and Batman and many chocolate Disney characters. I even saw an ad for "vegan chocolate" and I bet if I looked long enough I could find chocolate eggs that were filled with soy instead of gooey cream. But in all those displays, I never saw one chocolate cross. I suppose the store didn't want to risk offending anyone.

The message we get at this time of year is that we all get a second chance. Make the best of it. At least that's what McGregor says.

Try a New Recipe

I attended a Celebration of Life for a lady last week and I've always thought such an event is fitting so close to Easter when rebirth and resurrection are foremost in our minds. After the service over thick Nanaimo bars and homemade cookies, a couple of us were discussing that it is too bad we don't learn all the interesting things about people until they are gone.

We had learned that Louise was not only a very good baker but she was also an adventurous baker, often trying out her own recipes or altering old tried and true ones. Often her failures would be plunked on the counter and the family would eat it out of the pan and she would try again. "Why don't you just stick to the recipes?" she was asked. Well there is no adventure in always doing that is there?

As youngsters we are given the Recipe for Life and we are told that if we follow each step in order and add the proper ingredients in the described portions at the right time we will be a success. We all know half-baked people who never paid attention to those instructions but for the most part most followed pretty close to the family recipe.

But a lot of us will admit that some of the most adventurous and memorable times of our lives were when we decided to put that book away and make it up as we went along. We tried something new, we took a different path, and we took a chance.

One of my favorite posters says: "A good friend will bail you out of jail but your best friend will be sitting in the cell beside you saying, "Wasn't that the best night ever?" Now I'm not saying we should do something illegal but when we have always followed the recipe, even a minor deviation can be bold or risqué, and oh so exciting.

We went on a tour to Hawaii long ago. We were given an itinerary for the week and for the first two days we travelled with sixty people, we toured sights with sixty people and we ate with sixty people.

On the third day we slept in on purpose, left the itinerary on the dresser and rented a VW Bug convertible. With no map we took off on our own tour. We met locals and bought souvenirs at half the price, stopped when we wanted and had a picnic lunch on an isolated beach all to ourselves.

We didn't get back until after dark and we felt like rebels. We were sunburned and tired but we enjoyed the jealous looks of our travelling companions as we shared the spontaneity of our day. That was many years ago but that one day is the only thing I remember of that week.

I'll be the first one to admit that I should have referred to my recipe book a little more often and I've had my share of failed experiments but I pity the folks that arrive at the end of the line and heave a deep sigh because they never varied from their ingredients.

Maybe just for one day, make it up, add some new spices to your life, blend them into your day, turn up the heat a bit and see what happens. You can always clean out the pan and start over again tomorrow. At least that's what McGregor says.

Springtime and Easter

The four-day Easter weekend is a welcome break. The fact that it comes later this spring will surely be a boon for the hardware and gardening stores as folks hope the skies will clear and the temperature warms up so we can finally can finally start working outside.

I need that warm sun to coax me outside. After all, when there is hockey, baseball, golf and curling on the TV all at once, you don't feel quite as guilty sitting inside channel surfing when it is pouring rain.

Easter arrives with its promise of rebirth. We can read the magical story of the resurrection and take comfort and hope from that message or we can watch everything around us coming back to life and feed off the energy that brings.

We can imagine all those bulbs buried in the dark all winter and now beginning to push the rocks and dirt away from their caves and come back to life. We can find ourselves opening our doors and heading out into the sunlight once again to rake and clean and sweep away the darkness of the winter.

We look for signs to reinforce the messages of the Bible and yet sometimes we look too hard. Sometimes we look for such dramatic miracles that we miss the little ones happening around us all the time.

We often struggle with what to tell our children or grandchildren these days. Trying to implant our ideals on to them can be met with resistance sometimes. But it is important that they hear all sides of the story so that when the time comes, they can make up their own minds.

A friend of mine was surprised one morning when her little one asked her where the sunshine came from. She blurted out that "Mother Nature" brought the sun rather than the scientific explanation. Sometimes a simple explanation is the best. A least that's what McGregor says.

Jim McGregor

All about Sunshine

A sunbeam kissed my little girl
On the way to school today;
She asked, "Who brings all the sunshine?"
In a very innocent way.

How should I answer this I thought?
She took me by surprise;
I always have her answers
And she thinks that I'm so wise.

"Mother Nature brings the sunshine,"
Was what quickly came to mind,
But I knew that soon the answers
Would be more difficult to find.

Should I tell her the universe exploded,
That the sun's a fireball
And we go around it once a year
And it warms us one and all.

Or should I tell her God created us
And each day He sends the sun
To sustain all His creations
Because He loves us, everyone.

Maybe there is time, I'll wait,
And when her lessons are all done,
She'll make her mind up for herself,
But for today, Mother Nature brought the sun.

Finding the Oasis

At the end of a long day, travellers of old would seek out a quiet spot to rest. It was unusually the place where the wells were deep and cool and the water from within would quench their thirst and replenish their strength.

As we travel our incredible journey, we encounter people from time to time who just such an oasis in our desert. They have within them a heart where we can draw words, find calm or seek peace that will satisfy the thirst of our spirit and replenish the strength of our soul.

My Mother was that person. Like most mothers when were in need of comfort, a kind word, or a gentle blessing you would do well to find her for your place of solace.

She loved to write and I am blessed that she passed that down to me. She wrote letters and enjoyed getting written letters in return. Her poetry was always from her heart. Her handwritten words in a simple blank card would prepare friends or family for a visit to the hospital or speed their recovery on their return home.

She would write welcomes to the change of the seasons and poems rejoicing in the wonderful miracles that are spread out in front of us daily. While we complained about ice and snow covered roads, she wrote about the majesty of the snow covered Golden Ears that she could see from her balcony, reminding us that, regardless of the weather, "this is a day that the Lord hath made, rejoice and be glad in it."

She would welcome you as a new friend with a small poem of hope for the future or, if you were leaving, you would get a card with a prayer that would put your travels in the hands of the Lord.

In the early morning hours, with a cup of tea at hand, rhymes would flow easily from her pen to become hymns of hope and praise sung to the rafters of her new church. In the calm of the evening verses were composed to celebrate anniversaries or remember times and people who had passed before.

A stunning sunset would inspire words that would become a fundraiser with no compensation for her other than feeling the warmth of doing something to benefit others. There was no sounding brass to announce her accomplishments but rather a tinkling chime to let you know she had passed by your way.

We are allowed to mourn her passing, but only for a while, as she would not want anyone to "make a fuss". After that, we have to pick up where she left off. We have to be the one who writes the letters and makes the phone calls. We have to be the one who welcomes strangers and prays for the sinners. She would like that.

"Keep making new friends as you travel through life so you will never be left alone." At least that's what Peggy McGregor says.

Moms Do It Right

It is that special time of year when we get to put our mothers up on a pedestal, shining in the spotlight. Of course she will have to dust off and wipe down the pedestal and probably show us where we put away the spot light last year but, we'll do our best to give her a break for one day.

When the going gets tough, like this mini recession we're in right now, it is mothers that pick up the slack, tighten the belt, and find the extra potato or a tucked away ten-dollar bill. It is mothers who should be flown to Ottawa as advisors when the economy stumbles.

Mother Nature is barely keeping her head above water with global warming. Mother Hubbard is certainly going to find bare cupboards these days. What about the Old Woman who lives in the shoe with all those kids? She can't spank them and put them to bed hungry these days. As a matter of fact, here is what she would probably face today.

The East Side Tenants Association (ESTA) staged a protest at the site of a proposed athlete's village today after Olympic organizers unveiled a plan to demolish a row of low-income dwellings to make room for a condo development.

One of the dwellings to come down is the very recognizable Old Shoe occupied by the Old Woman. The Old Woman took over the dilapidated 19th century boot when she immigrated from England and found she had so many children, she didn't know what to do. The Old Woman was furious.

"These heels have no souls!" she shouted. "Can they not see how hard I have worked to make this place livable? Last spring I put in a new vinyl tongue to keep out the rain and the wind and we recently had the laces tightened for security."

"This is another blow in a series of decisions designed to evict these people," stated Ima Gainstit, the spokesperson for ESTA. "Last month they closed down the local food bank."

"I had to feed my children broth without any bread," said the Old Woman. "They all started fighting and screaming so I had to beat them all soundly to put them to bed and sure as God made little green apples, Children's Services showed up at my door."

When asked where she would go, the Old Woman shrugged. "There are some cheap flats out in the valley but I don't want my children growing up surrounded by loafers," she sighed. "It's sad you know, with a laminate insole and a rebuilt arch support, that shoe could sustain our family for years; it will be sad to see it brought down."

The Mayor stated, "The Old Boot should have been turfed long ago. But we tread lightly and don't want to step on anyone's toes. We want to put our best foot forward and leave a clean footprint for the future."

I'm sure The Old Woman will find a new place to live. She will clean it up and make it safe and warm. She will find schools and day care in the area; she will make it work.

I'm sure her children will have clean clothes, food in their tummies, and plenty of hugs and kisses. Moms always make things right; it's the basis for their job description. Make her one day a bit special. At least that's what McGregor says.

Mothers Are Influential and Inspirational

I was checking the web for an idea for a Mother's Day column. I found a conference touting it was, "The ultimate gathering of the world's most influential women." There were seven speakers listed there, a great source of inspiration I thought. However a further check of their bios revealed only one of the presenters was a mother.

Now, I'm not saying you have to be a mother to be influential or successful but I do believe motherhood experiences could have added to their presentations. For instance, one lady spoke on "The Secrets of Successful Women Investors." As a high level financial editor she no doubt knows where to put your money to double it or more.

But has she ever saved from her part time job for a trip to Disneyland? Had she had the experience of keeping the cupboards full of groceries, the kids drawers full of clothes, run the household and still had extra money hidden in her purse, her jewelry box, or a jar somewhere, she may have added some very valuable tips on successful money management.

A "Stress Management Expert" spoke on how to "Lighten up and reframe your thoughts" to relieve stress. If she had ever been up all night with child number one screaming with an earache only to have child number two wake up and start teething, her suggestions of taking time for yourself with a spa treatment may not be applicable here.

A lady recognized as a "Warrior Philosopher" spoke on "Strategic Thinking – Do Less, Achieve More". Ok, now let's put her in the strategic position of getting one child to baseball, one to piano and one to the orthodontist, in three different parts of town ten minutes apart and see if she can still "use eastern wisdom to solve life's ever-changing challenges."

How about the lady giving the Leadership/Motivation seminar? It was dealing with "Handling Outrageous Acts and Everyday Rebellions". She could probably benefit from a few years of trying to get teenagers out of bed, dressed, and off to school five days a week. The constant repeating, "Because I'm your mother" as an answer to almost anything, would not only clarify leadership but instill motivation as well.

A fashion model who survived the Boxing Day tsunami was speaking on Overcoming Adversity and how she made it back to the cover of Vanity Fair after serious injury. Admirable no doubt, a true survivor, but if she had ever had the flu the same time as the rest of the family but "overcame adversity" to empty the puke bowls, change the sheets, wipe the bums and make soup for her sick husband, helping the less fortunate in the world may take on a new light.

One of those sacrifices these ladies made was children and I won't speculate on how or why that came to be, but we can be thankful that our mothers become experts at all of the above. At least that's what McGregor says

Tools for Motherhood

A couple of items crossed my computer screen this past week that I thought may help me write a column for Mother's Day. Neither one was related to the other intentionally but they did tweak my imagination.

First, I saw an ad for a book titled, "The Modern Mother's Handbook: How to Raise a Happy, Healthy, Smart, Disciplined and Interesting Child, Starting from Birth." The Publisher's notes advise us in less than 60 minutes Mom will learn how to feed her children, teach them to sleep properly and how to play with other children so they will grow up to be smart, healthy and disciplined.

All of this information is contained in one book and not only does it tell you how to keep your sanity, but it tells you what Dad's job should be as well.

Wow, you can learn all that in sixty minutes, what a time saver that would be. I know my Mom didn't have a lot of spare time raising all us kids and keeping house but if she could have read a book like that before she had her first child, I'm sure raising her and the next five would have been a piece of cake.

The second item I saw was a picture of a wooden spoon accompanied by the question, "Other than serving food, what else was this used for in your house growing up?"

Now the connection I made is that because the mothers of my era growing up didn't have that sixty minute handbook to read, they had to find other ways of coming up with "no nonsense actionable advice to raise a happy, healthy, smart, disciplined and interesting child."

When Mom didn't have time to sit down and read advice books, and when the wooden spoon was hanging right there, handy, she could develop healthy eating habits in her kids, teach the rules for playing, and set bedtimes very quickly and efficiently.

There is a major debate about punishing children by spanking or hitting and I think we all agree it is good that that all of that is no longer socially acceptable, but has the pendulum swung too far the other way? I read a quote, "I was spanked as a child and developed a life-long psychological condition called, respect for others."

My tiny, sweet mother could get all three unruly sons with one swing of a fly swatter and we knew that if that plastic web came off she would still have the wire in her hand. We learned very quickly to be happy, disciplined, interesting children.

Apparently Duchess Kate read the handbook so we know our future King will probably never have a royal spanking and will grow up to be a kind and caring King.

I'm sure that bodes well for the British Empire. I'm also sure that the Queen had thoughts about taking a fly swatter to Charles a couple of times.

But the harshest tool any mother has ever used against a child is when she quietly says, "You've disappointed me." Nobody ever wants to disappoint their Mom.

This Sunday is Mother's Day. Do not disappoint your Mother. At least that's what McGregor says.

A Mother's Fashion Sense

New research has revealed that women with daughters tend to be more stylish than mothers of sons; a fact partly due to the style advice their daughters offer as they get older. It seems mothers seldom consult their sons on style advice.

"Women who don't have daughters may become less interested in style as they grow older but having a daughter, who is conscious of her own style, may keep alive her interest in looking great," comments psychologist Honey Lancaster-James.

There were both sons and daughters in my house when we grew up. I had never really thought about my mom's fashion sense or how she dressed when we were kids, so I closed my eyes and tried to visualize my mom at home and what she was wearing. The only image that seemed to come to mind was an apron. My mom always seemed to have an apron on.

Aprons were amazing garments. They held everything from cleaning rags to clothespins and seemed to be a uniform that signified our mom was a professional homemaker.

Try as I might, I can't recall my mom looking like June Cleaver or Loretta young wearing pearls or earrings at the dinner table. I don't remember her in slacks or shorts either. I don't think I ever saw my mom in high heels or running shoes and now this is starting to bother me because I must have seen her wearing something.

I do recall, the kids' clothes always came first. I'm sure that was same in many homes. She would mend her own clothes so we could have grad suits or grad dresses and we all went back to school in new clothes and shoes every fall. I wonder what she was wearing as we trotted off in shiny blue jeans and button down collars. I guess I was too absorbed in my own fashion sense to even notice.

In 60 years of dressing for the public eye, the Queen has never put on the wrong dress or the wrong shoes and people would only comment if she were wearing something out of place. Maybe it was the same with Mom. Maybe she just always had on the appropriate clothing for whatever she was doing at the time so we just accepted it.

If we had come home from school one day and found her in tight blue jeans with a blouse knotted around her waist and scampering around in saddle shoes, we would have taken notice alright and we would have said, "Mom, you are not going out looking like that!"

Because she had taught us that if our clothes were clean and covered every inch of our skin, we were ready to go out in the public. She made sure our clothes protected us from the sun and kept us warm and dry in the winter, even if I did take off my hat with the earflaps as soon as I got around the corner.

Of course with a family of six, there was always the financial concerns that dictated Mom's wardrobe. Even medicine for the cow would trump a new pair of shoes for Mom. But we never heard complaints.

Maybe I can't remember what she always wore, the important thing was that she was always there.

Happy Mother's Day. You mothers have earned your special day of recognition. At least that's what McGregor says.

Mother's Day Gifts

Are you still in search of the perfect Mother's Day gift? I heard that a liquor store displayed a sign, "Don't forget to buy your mom a bottle for Mother's day; after all, you were the reason she started drinking in the first place!" Maybe not the best sentiment nor the best suggestion to recognize someone so special, but we do try to choose the perfect gift for her each year.

I came across a chart listing the Top Ten Gifts for Mother's Day. From 10 up to 1 they were: flowers, candles, gift cards, gift basket, home spa treatment, home décor, chocolate, plants, perfume and a massage, pedicure, manicure day.

Certainly any one of those gifts will show your love and get you a hug. Any mother's home or apartment should be a blend of aromas and fragrances on Mother's day. The blossoms on the plants and the scented candles start mixing with a waft of the perfume and the essences from the gift baskets. We all have memories of our moms or grandmas homes and a whiff of something can transport us back there in an instant.

But some other research into Mother's Day gifts brought out a different Top Ten. I asked some mothers what their most memorable Mother's day gifts were and very few of them can be purchased at any mall or retail store. The question was usually met with a moment of thought then the smile of recognition as the image came into view.

"I got a small clay bowl, painted blue with Mom and a heart scribed into the bottom." I can remember making those with delicate care and using a toothpick to write with before the clay dried, then trying to remember what Mom's favorite color was. It seems to me, no matter what color we painted it, and Mom said that was her favorite.

"The cards, the handmade cards written in with crayon and the stick family inside; I still have most of them. I could just never seem to throw them out." We all took our time, using our best printing and intricate drawing with our tongues sticking out, making sure it was something Mom would like. It always got put on display and stayed there for days before being packed away.

"I loved the breakfast in bed. Listening to the commotion in the kitchen and the argument outside the bedroom door about who was going to carry what. Everybody sitting on the bed, and that was best." Sure we had to scrape the burned toast and the eggs were a bit runny and the tea was barely warm, but Mom said everything was 'just right.'

"Just having everyone over for the afternoon and staying for dinner. I always loved the noise, the chatter, hearing stories about school or sports and watching them grow up." Sure we all brought something so Mom wouldn't have to work but it wasn't long before the apron was on and she was at the stove or the sink. But we did make an effort to clean up before we left.

So there are two lists to choose from. One involves spending money; one involves spending time. Flowers wilt, candles melt, and chocolate disappears. It seems the personal touch, the time invested, the phone conversations, and the laughter linger well into the future and provide lasting memories.

Remember, she doesn't throw the important stuff away. At least, that's what McGregor says.

It's a Good Thing that Moms Worry

As a mother and her son were leaving a restaurant the other day, he gave her a hug and said, "You worry too much, Mom!" Holy smokes, where would be if moms didn't worry, if they didn't fret and stew and wring their hands? What would our lives be like if moms didn't agonize and lie awake until everyone was home? What if moms didn't wrap their fears and anxieties for us in their prayers or scold us and counsel us for our own good? The world would be a mess if moms didn't worry.

If moms didn't worry about schedules how would kids get to school on time or families get to church? Moms know that team pictures are at 10 AM at City Park and the game is on the same day at 2 PM at Milner. If moms didn't worry about how we smelled or how we looked, hockey socks and gloves would rot in hockey bags and baseball uniforms would be one huge grass stain by the third game of the season.

Moms know when the dentist and eye appointments are and that the orthodontist is in a different building than the regular dentist. If moms didn't keep track of how often we practiced there would be a lot less singers and gymnasts and many fewer pianists, violinists and trombonists.

If moms are going away for a day or two, they worry enough to leave casseroles, lasagnas, desserts and clean laundry. They phone to check up and toss and turn in that bed away from home. Dad can be gone for three days and no one notices, but mom worries about his flight or his drive, what he's eating, and how much sleep he's getting.

Remember when you used to come home after midnight? You could usually guarantee two things, Dad was sound asleep and mom was up. She had to stay up to worry if that boy was getting you home when he promised or if you took your girlfriend home when you promised. She had to worry if you were going to be up in time to get to work the next day and what would the neighbours think about someone coming home so late.

I suppose it all started when she found out she was going to be a mom. There was a lot to worry about then. What were the right foods to eat, how much exercise should she get? Would there be weight gain or morning sickness, would the baby come premature or would it be overdue? It's odd isn't it when the father says, "WE are going to have a baby." His life doesn't exactly carry the same worries over the term of the pregnancy.

Yes, moms know when there is trouble at school or on the team or in the marriage. They sense our medical concerns and they intuitively know when something is wrong no matter how far away we are from them. They will quietly agonize over our trials and tribulations until they can nervously broach the subject at what always seems to be just the right time. That's usually just before Dad says, 'Huh, what's this all about?'

Happy Mother's Day to all the mothers out there, and thanks for all your prayers and encouragement. Mom, I'd take you out to dinner on Sunday, but I know you'd worry about missing the Canucks game. At least that's what McGregor says.

Mother's Day Breakfast

Whenever we have a church supper, I am always impressed with the ladies in the kitchen during their preparations. They are like contestants on Dancing with the Stars as they glide and twirl between the stoves and counters, deftly transferring hot pans and bowls from one strategic spot to another. Before long, their well-oiled machine has coordinated a culinary masterpiece that steams a welcome from the buffet table.

So when the President of our council declared, "The men are going to prepare a Mother's Day breakfast" I volunteered to help in the kitchen, after all, how hard could cooking breakfast be?

I arrived as instructed just before 7:30 AM. I could smell the bacon frying as I approached the front door. As I went in, it looked a bit hazy in the lobby and the bacon smell was more pronounced as I headed for the hall. I peered through the haze and could barely see three figures in the kitchen. In my other life as a firefighter, my instincts would have been to don a breathing apparatus, drag these poor fellows to safety and give them CPR. However, I was greeted a cheery good morning by the smoky chefs and we chose to turn on the fans and open the doors and windows instead.

A homemade griddle was on the stove and the pancakes were coming off like an assembly line. Bacon was piled deep in a couple of frying pans and sausages were sliding into the oven. I was given the task of slicing watermelon, washing strawberries, and putting the three types of muffins onto the plates.

As more and more bowls and platters and trays were filling with food I asked, "How many mothers are we expecting?" But we kept cooking and slicing and peeling and mixing until we had used every plate, platter, and pot in the kitchen. Every utensil had been used for some function, whether it had been designed for that use or not and we were now finding pans of bacon that had been "warming" in the back of the stove for quite some time. We were not exactly working like a well-oiled machine but there was grease. But if we started to slip on the greasy floor, a patch of syrup would stop our slide.

We did have one of the ladies supervising us, saying things like, "That pan will be hot," or, "has the coffee been started?" Before long the tables were set, the fruit and muffin buffet was ready and the people started to arrive. We offered eggs any style as long as they were scrambled. We had three colors of bacon, black from the back of the oven, pink, still oinking until it was zapped in the microwave and of course, crisp golden brown.

The hall was alive with chatter and laughter as grateful moms, grandmas and families enjoyed a breakfast they didn't have to prepare. Some came back for seconds and two young boys took care of our concerns about too much inventory. The flapjacks were going like hotcakes and we hurried to keep up with the scrambled egg demands. I'm not going to report on the clean up other than to say some pans were taken home to be pressure washed.

A bold proclamation had yielded positive results and what had started out somewhat scrambled had ended sunny side up. At least that's what McGregor says.

Father's Day Memories

Fathers have it pretty tough. "Wait until your Father gets home." "When your Dad finds out…"

I saw a bumper sticker that read: "If you want your kids to grow up as good as you did, you have to be a tough as your old man was." Yes, society decrees that Dad has to be the tough guy, the disciplinarian. It's not until we're parents ourselves that we find out about the behind closed door meetings where fathers are given their daily instructions.

My dad was a milkman, up and gone early in the morning peddling milk for Seal-Kap Dairy, Hillside Farms, Jersey Farms, and eventually Dairyland. He missed three days of work in thirty years, and that was a tough act to follow. Our blood had to be oozing or bones protruding before we could miss a day of school. There was not much one on one time and I recall a twinge of jealousy when I came to pick up my son one day and found him and my dad, playing hockey in the driveway.

But there were a few memorable summer days when I got to go with Dad on the milk truck. Leaving home in the dark, loading the truck, covering the bottles with wet burlap sacks and ice and, it was so quiet. The rule seemed to be that no one spoke for the first few hours. The customer's orders were on the pages of the route books so you didn't have to be told, and the only sound for quite awhile was the tinkle of change emptying from the glass bottles. Imagine leaving money in a glass bottle overnight on your doorstep.

As the morning wore on and the traffic increased, the spell was broken and we settled into the day. Stopping on a side road for lunch included sandwiches and chocolate milk, but still very little conversation.

Dad was not a writer or a talker but the lessons of duty, responsibility, and honesty were taught loud and clear in the silence of those mornings. He spoke at times of driving the milk wagon for his aunt's dairy in Borden Ont. when he was younger and his lyrical memories of those early mornings are the ones I'll share in the quiet hours of this Father's Day.

If your dad is still part of your life, give him a hug, a handshake, or a phone call. If he's not, give him a few quiet minutes of your day; he'll be listening.

Remember, any man can be a father; it takes someone pretty special to be a Dad. At least, that's what McGregor says.

Milkman's Meloday

Clip, clop
Clip, Clop
The rhythm starts with the horse's feet;

Creak and rattle,
Creak and rattle,
Wagon wheels pick up the beat;

Jingle, jangle,
Jingle, jangle,
Harness chimes with hitch's moves;

Clinking, tinkling,
Clinking, tinkling,
Bottles keeping time with hooves;

Dogs barking,
Rooster crowing,
Morning birds are singing sweet;

Milkman whistling,
Sleepers stirring,
The song of an early morning street.

Father's Manual

Let's say it's time to leave the hospital with the new baby, your first baby. The baby's mother has been given copious advice on everything from breast-feeding to diet, how to handle depression or anxiety and dates for follow up examinations. What does the father get? Nothing. No one hands him an owner's manual or an instructional DVD, they just smile and say, "Good Luck!"

You wouldn't walk out of a car dealership without a manual. You wouldn't buy a new saw or lawn mower without some explanation of what to do if there was suddenly a loud squealing noise or a terrible smell. At least you would be given a 1-800 hotline number to call if your new item wasn't living up to your expectations, not to mention a return policy. But once you've strapped that new baby into the car seat, you are the father and you are flying by the seat of your pants.

Even your own father is not much help. I'm sure in a perfect world, your Dad would put on a pot of coffee and say, "Come sit down over here son, let's talk about your impending fatherhood and see if I can't guide you through this exciting phase of your life!" It's more like a pat on the back with the phrase, "Well, you've got your work cut out for you now, boy!" This is really more of a warning rather than anything instructional.

Fathers have no guidebook to tell them what to say when any and all of life's day-to-day trials come along. We know we're supposed to run along beside the bike when the training wheels come off but there is no chapter on what to say when they crash and the pain and the tears come so easily. Dads suddenly realize that there are many more sets of training wheels to come off over the next few years and there is bound to be scrapes and tears every time. Broken engines fix easier than broken hearts.

When they don't make the team, what page is that answer on? When they cut and dye their hair and get piercings in the grossest places, where does Dad look in the book so he can say the right thing? When they graduate, leave home, get a job, get married, buy a house, there should be page after page written on how Dad can express his feelings.

It's not that dads don't want to say something; they just don't want to say the wrong thing. It's not about lack of love, just lack of timing. But if Dad could pull that owner's manual out of the glove box or the work bench drawer, thumb through to the appropriate page, boy, he could be right up there with the world's greatest philosophers.

That's one of the reason's Grandpas seem so much smarter. They don't hesitate to give advice or long warm hugs. They have learned that the answers are not written down and in the past maybe they hesitated too often. Now when the chance comes, they know what they should have said all along.

In reality, if they did write an owner's manual for Dad, each page for each situation would simply say, "Give them a hug, then leave for two hours and let Mom sort things out."

Most dads do pretty well, considering the lack of instruction they get. At least that's what McGregor says.

Fathers Don't Want to be Involved

Here is a thought for Father's Day from a Family Counseling website: "Children with involved, loving fathers are significantly more likely to do well in school, have healthy self-esteem, exhibit empathy and pro-social behavior, and avoid high-risk behaviors including drug use, truancy, and criminal activity."

I guess I'm just not clear on the use of the word "involved." Historically, fathers are shadowy figures that live in the house that have the final say on important things without ever have been involved in the issue at all.

Be honest now, how many of you actually ever went to your father and said, "Hey Dad, I'm having this relationship issue at school; can you turn off the TV so we can talk about it?" Your dad would have gone straight to the bathroom.

Fathers don't like anything that is going to upset the status quo and they don't want to get involved in anything new, controversial, or romantic and certainly not in anything that is going to involve someone ultimately crying.

Unless the solution is that your father can yell at someone or threaten them in some way, they are not interested.

For example, last week there were two news stories about a mother duck trying to get her babies to a water source in downtown Vancouver. Did we see Father Duck in any of these stories? No, because getting the kids from one place to another is Mom's problem. Dad already has his ducks in a row and he is busy doing those things that dads do when they are not home. We don't question that.

No doubt when Mrs. Duck caught up with him she told him they were on TV twice, on the six o'clock news. Dad probably stopped preening for five seconds and said, "Oh really, and how much is that going to cost us?"

For Fathers, it always comes down to money. Comedian Jeff Foxworthy says, "All men eventually become their fathers; the minute my wife told me I was going to be a father, I immediately turned the thermostat down."

Statistics show that Mother's day is the world's most active day for long distance calls. Father's Day, not so much. Firstly, dads don't answer the phone and when you do get him on there and say "Happy Father's Day," he will say, "Oh thanks, did you want to talk to your Mom? She's right here." He knows you will start asking questions about dinner or visits or tell him something about the grand kids he won't remember long enough to relate to his wife, so it's better to just not get involved and hand off the phone.

If we ever did decide to get up the courage to involve Dad in some situation our first obstacle to approaching him after dinner was Mom saying, "Shhh, don't wake your father up." It's actually very cool being a Father, sort of like hibernation. You can wake up in your recliner and find the place clean and quiet and feel like you've slept all winter. Things have been looked after and they didn't ask you for help.

Asking Dad to comment on relationship breakups is like asking Mom to choose the new brake pads for the car. We all have our family roles to play.

Leave a nice card beside his chair and let him sleep; just don't involve him in anything. At least that's what McGregor says.

Lessons From Dad

About fourteen old classic car enthusiasts brought their vehicles to the parking lot of Harrison Point Seniors' residence last week. Now to be clear, the cars were old but the enthusiasts were, well let's say, experienced. The vehicles were from the twenties up to the sixties and each one was shined up and proudly on display.

When the residents came out for a look, each one of them had fond memories of trips they had taken or learning to drive or just the fun they recalled in the Model A or the big old DeSoto. I tried to pry out some racy stories but it appeared the code of the day was, "What happened in the rumble seat, stays in the rumble seat."

The drivers were treated to a fine lunch and Paola, the Activity Coordinator, asked us to go around the table and share where we were born, where we grew up and how we developed the love for classic vehicles.

Being that I was sitting about half a mile from where I was born, my story was the shortest, but the others placed at least seven or eight great column ideas in front of me.

I thought it was fitting, as Father's day approaches, that so many of the stories involved them working on tractors or trucks or cars with their fathers and how they learned the difference between the wrenches and screw drivers being "gofers" as Dad lay under the car.

Al shared the thought that he learned how the trouble light got its name. "My dad would often ask me to hold the light so he could repair something under the hood. No matter where I shone that thing, it was wrong and I was in trouble."

I remember holding the flashlight for my dad and if a wrench slipped and a knuckle got skinned, it was always somehow my fault because of the way I had been holding the flashlight. "For Pete's sake, hold that light steady so I don't keep dropping my tools." The day my little brother honked the horn while Dad was under the hood, really broadened our vocabulary.

Whether in the workshop, the field or the garage, it was always a proud and tense moment when Dad asked for your help. Would you live up to his expectations? Would you be a help, or a hindrance? Would you learn enough to be asked to help again or, better yet, be trusted with the task yourself next time?

In the later years, when Dad's hips and lungs would no longer support him, I was trusted with planting the vegetable garden. I was given "the stick." The stick was just a stick but it had three important notches on one end. Each was an indicator of how far apart certain rows should be planted.

As the vegetables grew, some rows you could still run the tiller between, they were the widest notch. Others you could hoe between and smallest were hand weeded. It was all about not damaging the crops, but it started with the stick and the twine at planting time.

I still have "the stick," but more importantly I gained the knowledge that measuring a project carefully at the beginning can make a big difference how it turns out in the end.

By far the best lesson from our dad was being there, setting examples, and letting us watch. At least that's what Mcgregor says.

Buying the Right Thing for Dad

Mark Twain is quoted as saying, "When I was a boy of fourteen, my father was so ignorant I could hardly stand to have the old man around. But when I got to be twenty-one, I was astonished at how much he had learned in seven years."

As Father's day rolls around again, no doubt plans are being made in many households on what is the best way to make Dad happy for at least one day.

Mother's Day marks the biggest day of the year for florists. I don't know if Canadian Tire keeps track of such things but I'll bet Father's day marks the biggest day of the year for sales of things for Dad's car that he will put in the trunk and never use.

The phone company tells us that on Mother's Day there is a significant increase in long distance calling and phone usage as everyone wishes Mom the best and spends some time catching up on family.

Most Dad telephone conversations on Father's Day go like this: "Hi Dad, Happy Father's Day!"

"Oh thanks, here's your Mom."

I recall phoning home one day and Dad answered the phone. I immediately thought something terrible had happened to Mom. Dad replied, "She's hanging clothes on the line, phone back in ten minutes."

What do you buy for a Father's Day gift? A friend shared, "One year I gave Dad a hundred dollars for Father's Day and told him "buy yourself something that will make your life easier." He bought jewelry for Mom."

If you are reading this on Friday, two days away from Father's day, and you haven't bought a gift yet, you're probably not going to put a lot of thought into it. What kind of dad is he? Is he active, out there golfing or biking or fishing? Or is he the "unbutton his pants, sit in the big chair and watch sports" kind of guy?

You have to know because buying the "easy chair dad" a fitness tracker is a huge waste of money. Maybe he's more suited to wireless headphones so he can listen to Buck Martinez announce home runs while tuning the rest of the world out.

A card is always nice but put some thought into it that expresses your personal relationship with your father. There is always the card with the fishing rod and reel on the front lying next to an old wicker creel and the verse inside says something like: "Dad, I think of you often and with love; you have shaped me and encouraged me."

Or, maybe your relationship is better marked by the card that shouts, "World's Greatest Farter!" and has a cartoon inside of a family holding their noses and a verse that says, "Dad, you leave me breathless!"

If your dad is still with you, make a fuss over him. If he's not, find a quiet spot to say thanks. Either way, he'll appreciate it. At least that's what McGregor says.

Sons and Daughters Have Different Approaches to Father's Day

As Father's day approaches, sons and daughters will view day from different perspectives. A hug from a daughter can be one of the most intimate and caring demonstrations of love between two humans. A hug between father and son is probably one of the most awkward acts any man will ever perform.

A daughter will put some thought into a gift for Father's Day. She will look at the new fashions, and may often try to introduce something new and daring into Dad's wardrobe.

She will spend a considerable amount of time at the card rack, reading the verses searching for the sentiment that best describes the relationship between her and Daddy.

A son won't usually spend that much time. Maybe punch Dad on the shoulder followed by, "Happy Father's day, Pop." If there is a card there will be no trace of a sticky verse that may include the word love.

Noted radio personality and philosopher, Garrison Keillor offers: "The father of a daughter is nothing but a high-class hostage. A father turns a stony face to his sons, berates them, shakes his antlers, paws the ground, snorts, runs them off into the underbrush, but when his daughter puts her arm over his shoulder and says, "Daddy, I need to ask you something," he is a pat of butter in a hot frying pan."

Of course, it is different when our children are small, when our sons have us up there on a pedestal with Spiderman, Batman, The Hulk and other super heroes. I still have some cards my sons made me in elementary school with hand drawn fire trucks or firemen on the front and amazing verses on the inside.

My friend Capt. Gerry Collins of the New York Fire Department was working on the pile of World Trade Center rubble a month after 9/11. The procedure was set that if a personal item was found, the location was marked and numbered and the item was bagged and the number and location was recorded.

If a body part was found an air horn would sound and a more intricate procedure was carried out.

Capt. Collins recalls one day when the air horn sounded. A rescuer hadn't found a body part but he had located a small clay ashtray. It was hand painted blue and scrawled inside were the words, "Happy Father's Day, Daddy." Amidst all that death and wreckage of twisted metal, it had survived, unscathed.

Strong men removed their helmets and wept.

Carlo Collidi, the author of Pinocchio writes: "Today at school I will learn to read at once; then tomorrow I will begin to write, and the day after tomorrow to cipher. Then with my acquirements I will earn a great deal of money, and with the first money I have in my pocket I will immediately buy for my papa a beautiful new cloth coat. But what am I saying? Cloth, indeed! It shall be all made of gold and silver, and it shall have diamond buttons. That poor man really deserves it; for to buy me books and to have me taught he has remained in his shirtsleeves...and in this cold! It is only fathers who are capable of such sacrifices!"

A man's children and his garden both reflect the amount of weeding done during the growing season." At least that's what McGregor says.

Building Bridges

As Father's day approaches I was in a discussion about chores and lessons learned at home. In a recent column I mentioned using a scythe and a few folks chimed in with some memories of their dad's or grandpa's prowess with the sharp, curved blade. My buddy Brian recalls that his mom used to say it looked like his dad was dancing as he cut through the long grass.

I could never swing it more than twice until the point of the blade stuck in ground and if I hit a rock, Dad could hear it no matter how far away he was and he knew the blade would need to be touched up with the stone.

I remember Dad working all the time, gardening, repairing, milking, mending fences or doing something with the animals. Maybe the six kids in the house had something to do with the time he spent in the yard. But we had our chores and they were expected to be done right and done on time. May be it was hauling pails of water to the trough, separating the milk and cream or filling the wood box. We never had the luxury to say, "I'll get it later!" Work first, play after, was Dad's rule.

I am approaching the age my dad was when he retired and remember him as being "old." He lived another twenty productive years and those were the years I got to know him, when we could sit and talk, work in his garden or trim his yard and share some stories. I recall a twinge of jealousy one day when I came to his place and saw him playing hockey in the driveway with my son. I couldn't recall him ever doing that with me.

Some words came to me when my grandson arrived just as my dad was leaving and reminded me it was my turn to pass things on. The seasons go round and round. At least, that's what McGregor says.

Hand in Hand

We cross the street, the hand in mine
Is warm and soft and small;
Fingers wrapped so tight on mine,
I feel so powerful and tall.

Beside the bed, the hand in mine
Is frail and pale and cold;
A smile comes with feeble squeeze,
I feel so scared and old.

Between them both, our hands reach out
Amidst our doubts and fears;
Our strength provides a common bridge,
A span to link their years.

Many stood, where we stand now,
We never saw their strain;
We held on tight as children do,
Oblivious to pain.

Did we learn kindness, or is it duty,
Which brought us here to-day;
Where generations on both sides,
Try hard to slip away.

It's your bridge you're constructing now,
So best build with love and care;
So when your time for crossing comes,
There's strong hands waiting there.

Dads Don't Belong in the Mall

A group of us from the Douglas Park Community School Society were cooking hot dogs at the City's Try-it Triathlon on the weekend. The event is exciting, well organized and carried off by some amazing volunteers. But when you look at the energy being expended by the participants, the safest place for an older crowd like us was behind the tables serving hot dogs and pop.

I approached a couple of young mothers I know who were waiting for their kids at the finish line. "What time do you two go out on the course?" I asked. They both looked at me with some disdain and one of them smiled sweetly and said, "When you are raising young children, every day is a marathon. You should write an article about that." There was very little humor in her voice so I was cautious in my reply.

The other lady spoke up and said, "No if you want a story idea, write about how useless husbands are in the child raising department. Our son is out there on the course today in shoes that are too big for him because his father took him shoe shopping yesterday. This morning, when we went to put them on, I noticed they were too big and I couldn't believe they didn't try them on."

I know the father in question here so I spoke to him later and he replied. "We were in the shoe section and I asked him what size his shoes were. He said four so we bought four. I figured he would know what size his shoes were." Father's make assumptions, maybe not always correct, but if our son knows his phone number and his address we are going to assume he knows his shoe size.

But there are some rules of life that young mothers have to learn. When shopping for kids, mothers are responsible for shoes, socks, underwear, pants and shirts. Fathers are responsible for sporting equipment.

A good example comes from my Little League coaching days. One of my T-ball players showed up with a new glove but I noticed he took it off to throw the ball. I figured out he was wearing the wrong glove. I explained to his mom that he needed a glove for his left hand. "What do you mean? I was in the sporting goods store and there were right handed gloves and left handed gloves and he is right handed." Some of those conversations can be quite challenging.

The bride buys dresses, flowers, caterers, the hall and the music. The groom rents a tux and shows up. Men buy cars and trucks and women choose paint and carpeting. Women buy kitchen cabinets and appliances, men buy beer.

Women don't feel comfortable buying a family vehicle because of a lack of negotiating experience, difficulty understanding auto jargon, or maybe a feeling that the dealership staff isn't taking her seriously. Exactly the same reasons you don't see men in lingerie shops.

There are basic laws of society and when they are violated, paint and carpets clash, and kids show up at sporting events in the wrong size shoes.

The young man finished his triathlon without stumbling or falling, the medal around his neck and the grin on his face told us the day was worth it. By the time school starts in September those shoes will be too small anyway. At least that's what McGregor says.

My Friend's Birthday

I'm going to help my friend celebrate her birthday; actually, she's one of my best friends. You know the type, a friend that you can neglect or ignore and yet, when the going gets tough, you turn around and there she is, ready to give you hand.

Her birthday is always on a long weekend and I will confess there were times when I used the occasion as an excuse to party the whole three days with absolutely no concern for her feelings, not giving much care to the mess I was making or who was going to clean it up. But, as they say, "too soon old, too late smart," so now when I get her invitation, I try to do something just a little distinctive to mark her special day.

She is such a gracious and giving lady. No matter how many people show up or where they come from, she welcomes them, she makes sure they have plenty to eat or drink, and if they need a place to stay, she just opens up another room. Her yard is always neat and tidy, a safe place to play; she is the perfect hostess.

I often forget how beautiful she is and too many times it has taken a perfect stranger or a visitor meeting her for the first time to remind me of what a looker she can be. Other times, it might just take a glimpse of her silhouette at sunset or opening the door in the morning and see her there waiting for me. She can still take my breath away.

I think part of the reason she turns so many heads is because of her fashion sense. No matter what the season, she always seems to find the perfect thing to wear. Many people wait for the spring just to see what new colors she is going to introduce each year, and she can drape herself in autumn hues that inspire even the most famous designer houses.

She is constantly being invited out; her social calendar is always full. She is always welcome wherever she goes and people are always glad to see her, the perfect guest. She is never loud, obnoxious or boastful, she never makes a scene and she will ask if they need help with the dishes before she leaves.

To compliment all that beauty, she has amazing grace. I have watched her time and time again, peacefully diffusing an argument or offering her skills to mediate disagreements among her neighbours. They respect her calm, caring attitude and always seem to listen to her quiet suggestions.

But I have learned not to confuse her kindness for weakness. If she is asked to solve a problem or work toward a solution there is no hesitation. She will roll up her sleeves, tie back her hair and get right to the task at hand, and, don't get in the way.

Recently, I was away for a few days and yet, when I returned there she was to meet me with a just a whispered,

"Welcome home." I smiled back, took a deep breath of fresh air and said to her, "Happy Birthday Canada!"

Don't just celebrate with her one weekend each year; celebrate her all year round.

Taken for Granted

Canada Day is here already. Most of us who are born and raised here are pretty smug, we take being Canadian for granted, we are, to say the least, comfortable. I spent a few hours at Community Day this past week and the mix of nationalities there brought out some interesting conversations.

I was listening to man who emigrated from Hungary with his family. He spoke of the opportunities and the open spaces and how clean it was. As he spoke, another woman mentioned that she felt immigration was OK but now it is getting out of hand, "we should do something about all the people we are letting in." He simply replied that immigrants are what makes Canada strong. I couldn't help but think that many young people died and are still dying to allow that kind of open conversation to take place in Canadian public parks. Openly sharing different points of view isn't something that's allowed everywhere.

Some people say emigrants are taking our jobs. Business owners tell me that Canadian youth won't cook fries, slice pizza, pick fruit, work in the mills or do anything that might be considered manual labor. They want cell phones, company cars, pension plans, and insurance; and they want it today. I heard one employer say that the problem most young people have with instant gratification is that it doesn't happen fast enough.

I spoke to a man setting up a cleaning service. He has an engineering degree from his country of origin but it doesn't qualify here. But he would rather clean other people's buildings than go back

As I watched the pipers I met an 86-year-old man from Scotland who came here in 1953. The last time he played the pipes was in a POW camp. When he got home he tried to make it work but his country was too "ravaged and ruined" and for his family's future he was advised to come to Canada. Can any of us imagine Canada being so ruined politically, economically, socially, or geographically that we would want to leave and do whatever we had to do to not have to come back?

That begs the question, where would you go? If you could no longer live in Canada, where is a better place in the world to live? We have elections in a few months and it's not likely hundreds will be killed trying to vote. We don't often have cruise missiles fired at us or roadside bombs or mines killing our children. We can drink water out of the tap, we can get basic medical attention for nothing. We throw out tons of edible food every day and the biggest common problem we face in Langley is that they changed the company that picks up our garbage.

We don't teach our upcoming generations to appreciate what they have been given. During my day at the park, I picked up at least six small Canadian flags that had been dropped on the ground. Our flag is not supposed to touch the ground. Do we still teach patriotism? The only place we consistently sing the national anthem is at sporting events. I'm afraid a whole generation will grow up thinking the last two words to Oh Canada are 'Go Canucks!'

I'm not worried about the aggressiveness of New Canadians, just the complacency of the old ones. Celebrate Canada Day, at least that's what McGregor says.

Spending Canada Day at Aldergrove Beach

We all enjoyed a fairly decent Canada Day weekend last week, not too hot to sunburn and not to wet to dampen events around the community. During a conversation about past long weekend activities someone mentioned that one of their favorite pastimes as a Langley kid was going to Aldergrove Beach on hot summer days.

Yes, there was a beach in Aldergrove, situated where the Aldergrove Lake Regional Park is now. If you walk west from the parking lot, there is a large expanse of gravel and some quiet trails. But there used to be a huge man-made lake on that spot and it was anything but quiet on a summer day.

The free pool was opened as "Aldergrove Beach" in 1963 by property owner Harry Keillor, and taken over by the Greater Vancouver Regional District (now known as Metro Vancouver) in 1969. It served as a close-at-home summer vacation destination for thousands of Langley and Abbotsford residents until it was shut down in 2011 because of new B.C. Public Health Act regulations that defined the "lake" as a public swimming pool requiring an operating permit. With a stroke of a pen, summer days were changed forever for many families.

The pool was a large oval surrounded by white sand that was perfect for spreading blankets or setting up lawn chairs. In the middle of the "lake" a four-inch pipe gushed cold water up in a fountain and a common dare was to swim out there and see how long you could hold onto the pipe.

You had to get there early. The parking lot and the beach filled up quickly and you wanted to find a spot where you get some sun, watch the kids, put your cooler and picnic basket under the shade of the trees and be not too far away from the toilets, changing rooms and concession stand. There was a floating dock in the middle and it was just deep enough to dive off although the signs told you not to. There was a roped off area for the little kids and often mothers would be yelling at bigger kids who were chasing each other around in the little kids area.

In the summer of 1969, the site was the location of the Aldergrove Beach Rock Festival. Fresh on the heels of Woodstock, many music festivals sprang up in small towns across North America. Some of the big acts at the three-day event were The New Vaudeville Band and Guitar Shorty, Black Snake and Trooper. Canadian singer Valdy, was inspired to write his hit song, "Play Me a Rock and Roll Song" after being heckled and booed for his folk songs on the Aldergrove stage. It was a big deal for us country boys to wander through the steady, heavy crowds, 25-30,000 people over three days, in the thick smell of pot, watching our old swimming hole being transformed into a rock concert.

I have no doubt many local families went there in the evening after a hot day in the fields for a quick dip to cool off. It was close by, it was free and you always recognized someone you knew at the little country swimming hole.

Somehow, no matter how much we had eaten, I always got talked into stopping at Dairy Queen on the way home, because a day at the beach always has to end with ice cream. At least that's what McGregor says.

Going to the Fair

I enjoy "people watching" and events like May Day, Community Days or Canada Day are perfect venues for this passive hobby. I smile at the children's excited cheering as the parade passes by or their squeals and screams on the amusement rides. I love to watch mischievous grandparents gleefully buying popcorn, ice cream or souvenirs for the grandkids and exhibiting ten times more patience than they ever did at these events with their own children.

The line ups at the local church hamburger booth or the service clubs chicken barbecue or pancake breakfast are amazing blends of conversation and interaction as strangers become neighbours for a short time just waiting for the onions to fry. It's all about family and down home simple fun and I believe if we had a weekly fair, it would always be well attended.

But I also enjoy preparing the venues. There is a gentle calm the night before or the morning of the event as the empty field is transformed. It's as if a Gypsy caravan has appeared out of nowhere. There is a special time just before the crowd arrives when you know everything is ready and everything is silent. The same can be said when it's all gone at the end of the day and you stand in the stillness with the grass and trees. Both times represent a feeling of accomplishment, a job well done.

After spending a few years in the school of hard knocks I came to the realization that the early morning, before you head for your daily fair, is the tranquil time to decide which rides you will go on today, which risks you will take and who you will trust to take them with you. You can decide who gets in for free and who and who has to pay. If they aren't smiling, don't let them in.

By making your choices in the hush of the morning, and maybe asking for some guidance along the way, you may just find it's a little more peaceful and rewarding when everyone has gone home at the end of the day. At least that's what McGregor says.

Gates Open at 10:00

Early in the morning
Before your carrousel is spinning,
When the horses haven't started
And the swings are hanging still,
Sit quietly and listen
As the flowers are unfolding,
Watch closely as the sunrise
Melts the mist upon the hill.

At the very start of day
Before your gates of thought are open,
When the crowds of worries line up
Preparing for your daily ride,
Look around and notice
All the things that are important,
Then before the day's confusion
Decide just who you'll let inside.

Before the rush has started
Before the seats have all been filled,
Make sure that only happy riders
Have bought tickets to your park;
Then sit back, enjoy the ride
Hear all the laughter there inside,
Until contented horses, tired swings
Are sitting silent in the dark.

The Disappearing Pumpkins

My pumpkin patch is gone. It has been tradition for the past 40 years that we all gather the week before Halloween, on a day close to my daughter's birthday, and have a celebration. When my dad had the farm, it was a time to trim and prune and gather deadfalls and create a large bon fire that would burn all afternoon and into the evening.

Relatives from the city would come out and stock up on vegetables from the garden and leave with a perfect jack o' lantern. Dad grew lots of pumpkins and gently turned them as they progressed so they wouldn't develop a flat spot.

We would make sure they had lots of water over the summer and the special treatment paid off come October. There was always one that flaunted early that it was to be the prize of the patch, and over the summer we would trim off extra shoots or vines so it got all the nutrients.

But we knew that we wouldn't get to have that big one for our Halloween doorstep. The city kids or the grandkids got to take that prize home. Dad always said "If you're going to give something to somebody, always give the best you've got." I have to admit that it was a few years before I realized he just wasn't talking about pumpkins.

Once the fire settled down, we'd break off some late corncobs and dig up some potatoes and toss them into the bottom of the fire and it wasn't long until we had plenty of roasted vegetables to go along with the hot dogs and s'mores.

Birthday cake, pumpkin pie and ice cream finished off the day and when the relatives had waved goodbye it was nice to sit with a mug of coffee, enjoy quiet conversation, and watch the glow of the embers guide us into the evening.

But after the farm was sold, the only one that had a big back yard was I so the annual event came to my place. I didn't have the plot or the patience for growing prize pumpkins so every year I would go to a local pumpkin patch, buy five or six so the kids could choose their own.

This year, I took the old truck out for a drive and headed for the farm. As I came to the corner, I noticed the farmer didn't have his big plywood "U-Pick" smiling pumpkin sign nailed to the fence. As I turned the corner it seemed I could hear that ominous scary movie music playing and I had a sense of foreboding.

I came to the end of the road and there it was, gone. No farmhouse, no barns, and certainly no five acres of bright orange pumpkins. There were curbs and paved streets. There was heavy equipment and piles of gravel. There was progress instead of pumpkins.

After an extended drive I found a new farm, surrounded by trees and fields and horses, for now, but who knew that pumpkins will soon be added to the endangered species list. It won't be long until clandestine farmers will be growing pumpkins hidden amongst the corn or I have to meet some guy in a dark parking lot and give him an envelope of cash and smuggle my treasures home.

When you're making your jack o' lantern, hoard those valuable pumpkin seeds. At least that's what McGregor says.

Choosing a Costume

I was going to a masquerade party last week and I was debating if I should "dress up" or not. I decided on just buying a black mask so I would still be part of the crowd and yet be able to slip it off easily as the night wore on.

I went in and out of costume shops and thrift store and big box stores looking for just a plain black mask with two eyeholes like the Lone Ranger used to wear. He wore that for years and no one ever figured out who he was and I only needed for a couple of hours.

There were thousands of costumes to choose from. They ranged in price from $19.95 to $100.00. I could buy or rent any kind of costume and be whatever or whoever I wanted to be but I just wanted a black mask.

No wonder we don't have many heroes around anymore. The Lone Ranger can't buy a mask, Superman no longer has phone booths to change in, and society has made it difficult for the superhero. Personally, I was always amazed that nobody could tell that Clark Kent wasn't Superman; I mean, really, just a pair of dark rimmed glasses for a disguise? At the very least Lois Lane should have figured that out.

In one store a mother had laid out four costumes on the floor for her six year old boy to choose from. Our choices were a ghost or a pirate for the boys and a ballerina or a princess for the girls. Basically, anything that could be made by mom at home. Studies show the average B.C. family today spends $90.00 on Halloween, more if they have more than one child.

The little boy in the store was having trouble making up his mind. I'm a grandpa so I thought I'd offer some advice. "The Ninja costume comes with a sword, I pointed out, "Yeah!" he exclaimed, "I want the one with the sword!" I thought maybe I would get a quick "thank-you" from Mom for helping but the look she gave me was more of "Mind your own business." But he got his Ninja costume.

The sword is an important part of that costume on the trick or treat route. He can poke his sisters with it until they get mad, a great Halloween memory for a brother. If someone has a hockey or fire helmet as part of their costume, he can "boink" them on the head with it until the helmet is wedged on tight or he can slay any number of imaginary ghosts or goblins that might spring from the dark cul-de-sacs.

He will have great fun until one of those adults loses it and grabs it from his hand saying, "That's enough of that bloody sword." Trick or treating can be stressful for parents.

Picking out a Halloween costume can be difficult and yet we put on a different costume every day. When we are getting dressed and ready to leave the house, who do we want people to think we are? Can we get through the whole day without anyone seeing who is really behind our mask?

I couldn't find the mask I wanted so I decided to go as something that strikes fear into all Canadians. I put on a suit and tie and went as a Senator. I hope your Halloween has more treats than trick. At least that's what McGregor says.

Trick or Treating

I have just looked out the window for the tenth time. It's still not dark. Mom says we have to make sure our chores are done and we've had dinner before we can go out trick or treating. Other people will still be eating and we don't want to disturb their dinner.

Our costumes are home made. Mine is an old white sheet with two eyeholes, the basic ghost costume. My little brother is a cowboy. We have a couple of old pillow cases for a loot bag and a flashlight that works if you fiddle with the switch and smack it once in a while. We are ready to go.

Our road is about one mile long and we will go to one end and work our way back. The first stop is Frost's where we will be asked to come into the kitchen and perform something before we get our treats. It takes way too long as far as we're concerned.

We go over to Sharien's and my brother's friend Bobby joins us and we head down the dark, unlit road with water filled ditches on each side. There is a moon but a Halloween moon is not there to guide you, it is there to provide shadows only.

We skirt past the old man's house with no lights on. We dare each other to run up and knock on the door but no one is that bold this early in the evening.

We arrive at Dyck's and Harold and Gordie join our troop and off we go. Going up the steps at Nicholl's house I trip on my sheet and fall on my bag. This promotes gales of laughter from the rest and now I can only see out of one eyehole.

Then we come to a decision. Lightfoot's have a long gravel driveway, do we go up there now or on the way back. We decide to go now and half way back down the drive way, the flashlight quits altogether, so I give it to my little brother to carry.

At Hickey's, we discover Russel and Dennis have gone out already so we'll find them somewhere on the way. We cross the road to Campbell's then up to Mrs. Harris' where we know her homemade caramel covered popcorn balls will be waiting on a tray cover with wax paper. We will have to perform again but the prize is worth the wait.

Down the road to Amundson's and Mrs. Ski's house then a dark stretch until we come to Hiebert's and then Muench's where we start to run into their kids and we turn back toward home. Now the group is large and noisy and the discussion is all about which house is giving out candies or Lifesavers and which ones are giving out raisins or apples.

I have stepped on my sheet many times and I no longer look like a ghost, just a kid with a white sheet around his shoulders, but we're almost done so who cares. It's time for the corn roast and fireworks.

This year the families will come to our place and the gather around a back yard fire with hot chocolate and coffee for the adults. Everyone has brought their fireworks and we fire them off to mark the end of a perfect evening. The only task left is to smuggle candy to bed.

Halloween was pretty simple back then. At least that's what McGregor says.

Halloween Memories

Trick or Treat! There is no better way to describe my Halloweens over the past thirty-five years. As a member of the local fire department my Halloween nights were a mixture of treats, sharing the early part of the evening with my kids in their costumes, then the tricks, spending the second half of the night chasing the true goblins of the community.

The afternoon of the big event or, maybe the night before was for carving pumpkins. Most years, just the basic Jack-o –lantern smile, the triangle eyes and nose, the jagged smile, the recognizable picture good old Jack would have on his driver's license. Occasionally, the knife would slip and an orange tooth would fall to the floor but you could jam that back into place with a toothpick, knowing full well Jack had no formal dental plan. Then as the kids got older we got fancier, with the patterns and the miniature saws to create intricate spiders or witches, but we always made sure there was at least one Jack.

Sometimes, we would spread the pumpkin seeds on a cookie sheet and bake them and if we didn't forget them, we had something to crunch on. If we did forget them, the smell of Halloween lingered in the kitchen for a day or two. We read a tip in an article suggesting we cut grooves in the lid of the pumpkin, sprinkle cinnamon or nutmeg in them, and let the candle send those wonderful baking smells wafting off your porch.

Creating costumes was exciting, limited only to the imagination. One year, when Star Wars was at its peak, (the first time around, in the '70s!) My wife found a pattern for Ewoks, the furry little extra terrestrial friends of Princess Leia. Much care went into their fabrication and the two kids set forth with their pillowcases in hand.

Soon everyone was saying, "What cute little teddy bears!" This wore thin with the kids after a few houses and eventually I would be standing on the road listening to my cute little daughter loudly exclaim on the doorstep, "We are not bears, we are Ewoks!"

Once back home we would check out the haul with hot chocolate and then I would head down for the fire hall, and wait. The fun of the evening soon wore off as the alarms started to come in. Mischief and vandalism, as garbage containers, empty buildings, schools, parked cars, all became targets. It wasn't long until the smell of pumpkin seeds and cinnamon were replaced with pungent fireworks sulfur and acrid black smoke.

While we waited at the hall, we would each put a quarter in the pot and draw a number to see which hall would get paged out next. On a full moon Halloween, you could make two or three dollars in quarters.

Some years, the weather was our best friend and the hooligans would go home wet and early. Other years we would wrap up the hoses and turn off the lights at three or four in the morning and count up the dollar losses the next day. Most firefighters don't have a lot of fond Halloween memories, but those Ewoks were cute!

Give thumbs up to the Police, Fire and Ambulance crews this week. They are all hoping for that perfect October 31st. weather forecast, clear and dry 'til 7:30 PM, rain like hell the rest of the night, at least, that's what McGregor says.

Trick or Treating Adventures

Over a couple of pumpkin spiced lattes, soon be replaced with eggnog lattes, some of us were discussing Halloween and reminiscing about trick or treating. Over the years, from our childhood and now with our children or grandchildren, the evening has changed.

It seems that back in our day, we all someone on our block who took on a more ominous aura around Halloween. There was a person who didn't participate, leave their porch light on or give out treats.

They were often referred to as "the mean old man" or "the mean old lady." Rumours would abound among the neighborhood children of strange sounds or occurrences coming from their house or yard and we would hurry past giving that evil place a wide berth. Except if you had smaller kids with you.

Then it was always fun to tell them they had to run up and knock on that darkened door or throw an egg at the spooky porch, telling them that we had done it when we were their age.

We had a man who lived alone on our street. Always wore overalls, drove a rusted old pick-up truck and never had anything to do with the neighbours. He had apple trees in his front yard that hung with fruit in the fall. It was always a dare to steal his apples.

The blackberry bushes in his back field seemed to have bigger and juicer berries than anyone else and we would sneak under the barbed wire like advancing Special Forces just to get a pocketful without being seen. And his house was always dark on Halloween.

To run into that evil place and grab an apple off the ground and jump back across the ditch on a dark Halloween night, shouting, "Mean old man, mean old man, run away as fast as you can," was the sign of ultimate courage.

In later years, taking my kids around in fully lighted neighbourhoods on smooth sidewalks didn't seem to have the same sense of adventure. One year, my neighbour and I took our two six-year-old boys on our planned route. At the point of no return where we were the furthest from our homes, his boy says, "Dad, when we get to the next house can you ask them if I can use their bathroom, I have to poop."

His Dad replied, "You know, I think that gives a whole new meaning to trick or treat, nobody wants a strange kid pooping in their toilet"

My son suggested, "Just squeeze you butt cheeks together when you walk until the feeling goes away." That seemed to work and it became a Halloween memory for the boys.

Today, kids can go to "organized" trick or treating in the mall or to planned parties where children exchange treats.

How boring is that? Is there going to be mean old people there? Is there going to be some jerk friend who will jump out from behind a tree and scare the daylights out of you? Will there be a long gravel driveway up to a creaky dark porch? Not many Halloween memories being made at the mall.

I think there should be one field set aside every year where city kids can sneak in and tip over an outhouse in the dark, complete with an old farmer in overalls who yells, "You kids get off my property." That's making memories. At least that's what McGregor says.

Standing On Guard

As we wade into November with the darker days and wetter weather, the only bright spots are the red poppies we all wear to commemorate our fallen soldiers.

This year, I suspect we will see an increased attendance at our Remembrance Day ceremonies due to the recent events in eastern Canada where we saw the death of two Canadian soldiers on our home soil. After all, wars happen in other countries, not here in Canada.

A historian friend sent me an article about a German submarine that operated off the east coast of Canada in 1918. The sub destroyed many freighters and fishing vessels by commandeering the boats, sending their crews ashore and scuttling the ships. Because there was no loss of life, there was very little national publicity.

The interesting part of the story is that the U-boat Commander had been given two orders. Firstly, to sever the trans-Atlantic telegraph cable that came ashore in Canso Nova Scotia, and secondly to cause as much "fearfulness" as possible for Canadians by bringing the European war to the shores of Canada.

Other than causing some havoc in the shipping lanes, the sub wasn't able to destroy the cable and obviously, most Canadians were not even aware of the attacks much less made "fearful."

After all, wars happen in other countries, not here in Canada.

But we must acknowledge that war has a different face these days and it is not as easily as recognizable as it used to be. Locking the doors and piling chairs against them may not be enough. We should start paying a little more attention. At least that's what McGregor says.

On Guard

The Unknown Soldier left his tomb
When he heard the terrible sound;
He glanced at the soldiers looking down
Then knelt by the man on the ground.

He cradled his head in his weary arms
Then smiled as he slipped away;
"Come with me," he said in a gentle voice,
"Our country has changed to day."

"Straighten your kilt and straighten your cap,
It's time to return to your post;
We must not leave; we must not hide
It's now we're needed the most."

"Your broken body has left the scene,
To be replaced by flowers and tears,
But I need you to march over me
To dispel your country's fears."

Your footsteps will echo from the Maritimes
Across the prairies to Pacific sand,
They will thunder in the hearts of your countrymen,
As they rise to make a stand.

"So stand fast your post young soldier,
Stand on guard for them and me;
For it's those of you, doing what you do
That keeps our country free."

Lest We Forget

A friend of mine shared her grandfather's WWI journal with me. He had spent a lot of time in Europe protecting our lifestyle and had chronicled some of his daily horrors. There is no glamour in a soldier's journal. Words like dysentery, gangrene, amputation and death, shout at you from the jagged handwritten pages. He talks of bone chilling cold, constant rainfall, mud and blood. I search for words like hero or victory and they are not there. It is a soldier's journal, not a general's and so the perspective of the battlefield is much different.

But then I came across a passage where he describes a scene of soldiers mustering, waiting for marching orders and suddenly the news travels down the line that the war is over. I took the liberty of finding a spot on a hillside in the south of France, just above where they were gathered. I sat quietly as his scene unfolded and tried to capture the words Private Balch had scribbled on those yellowed pages.

Even if it's just for a minute, stop this month, bow your head and give thanks for all who gave and continue to give their lives for our freedom. It is a debt we must continue to pay.

Let the Band Play

"Pack up boys we're movin' out!"
All he ever does is shout;
Give a slouch an extra stripe
And all he does is bitch and gripe.

"Drop the tents and stow the gear!"
God why not put a sniper near.
He's sending us from field and farm
To Satan only knows what harm.

So jump the ditch, and through the gate
And now it's hurry up and wait;
We'll muster here 'til God knows when,
Then wait for other broken men.

The voices up ahead give rise
We stand and stare we squint our eyes;
A rider hell-bent through the mud,
Horse's nostrils snorting blood.

What's that he yells, "It's over boys!?"
There's too much cheering, too much noise.
We've broken ranks, we start to run,
My God I'm hearing pipes and drums!

"It's over Boys" becomes a song
And every soldier sings along!
Helmets fly and young men cheer,
The strongest of us shed a tear.

The drums roll by and rumble on,
The Pipers pipe our memories home.
Each year that music brings to mind,
Boys who cheered, boys left behind.

Christmas Optimism

"Where are you going for Christmas this year?" That seems to be the most asked question right about now. For me, I have to bring a pie, a bag full of presents and show up at my son's place, and wait for the dinner call.

For some folks, this is their year to travel. Maybe they are daring and have booked a Christmas Eve flight, totally optimistic that the snow will be gone, the baggage handlers will have their raise and the plane will lift off on time. Surely the airport has fixed all those problems they had last year. Bacon and eggs Christmas morning at Tim Horton's on the departure level just isn't the same as sitting at your relatives in Edmonton trying to convert the wind chill factor.

But Christmas is all about optimism and hope. Like the people who have reservations on the ferries, for instance. Surely having a reservation means that you have a spot on the ferry, the ferry will leave the dock on time and you will arrive in Port Alberni just after noon. Unless of course, the winds come up or the engines go down.

Some are driving through the mountain passes to Kamloops or the Okanogan. They have snow tires and chains, a full tank of gas and a trunk full of confidence. The roads will be clear and sanded, the car will run smoothly, the kids will have out grown their car sickness and they will pull into Mom's driveway way ahead of schedule. They won't even allow thoughts of standing beside the car in a blizzard trying to read the instructions on tire chain box. Oh yes, Christmas traveling can be an adventure for sure.

But once you're there safe and sound it is the most wonderful time of the year shared with relatives that will either annoy you or entertain you. It has been said that two types of people show up at a family dinner. Those that help with the dishes and those who talk about their operations. But every visit is a bundle of memories waiting to be unwrapped.

On Christmas Eve, I'll gas up the truck and check the tires; that trip from Brookswood to Walnut Grove can be brutal at this time of year. At Least that's what McGregor says.

A Family Fruit Cake Recipe

Separate the brothers quickly
Or it's never going to set;
Mix the in-laws with the Grandpas,
But don't add the brandy yet!

Blend the Grandmas both together,
That's more sugar than you need,
Don't bring your sister to a boil
Or that's one less mouth to feed!

Toss in an aunt and uncle,
Sift in a cousin here and there,
Set your daughter's half-baked boyfriend
On the porch, to cool off there.

Once the glaze of rum appears,
Try keeping all those nuts awake,
Sit back, stir in the Grandkids,
That's the icing on the cake!

Home for Christmas

There is a line from a Christmas song that stirs up some memories: "I'm drivin' home for Christmas, to get my feet on holy ground." I like that. Everyone wishes to be home for Christmas or have all the family home with them. But as our families extend and add new twigs and branches onto the family tree, it becomes more difficult to have everyone gather in one spot, but when they do and they're together, warts and all, it surely seems like holy ground.

In my Christmas file I have a black and white photograph imprinted Dec. '63 on the bottom. My three brothers and I are sitting on the living room floor and my older brother, home on leave from the air force, has a set of dice and is showing us how to shoot craps. This is certainly not a Christmas tradition my mom wants to start in a good Christian home and even though no money is changing hands, the guilty look on our faces reveals that we being naughty, not nice.

I remember the excitement of hearing our big brother was coming home for Christmas that year. He pushed an old '55 Chevy through the prairie snow from Gimli Manitoba and the stories of his trip were just as exciting as the air force tales he told around the table. I'm sure there must have been a sense of peace for my parents to have the noise and the confusion of everyone home even if Mom did run through all four names whenever she was trying to talk to one of us.

Other years maybe it was Grandma Cole coming from Edmonton for the holidays. That would mean a trip down to the CN station in Fort Langley to meet the train. The blackboard inside the office would tell you if the train was on time or not. No computer screen or data link, just the chatter of the telegraph and the chalk from the stationmaster kept you informed.

We would peer eastward down the tracks until we could see the big headlight in the fog and eventually hear the train whistle. Once it ground to a stop, the porter would swing out, place the step stool and offer his hand to Grandma to help her to the platform. We would lift the big black suitcase from the baggage cart, knowing it was full of presents, scotch mints, and humbugs. Toast with cheddar cheese is always Christmas with Grandma.

Sometimes the visitors didn't travel far. Uncle Bob and Aunty Marg were close and whenever they pulled in the driveway, it felt like they were coming home for Christmas. My uncle enjoyed the party atmosphere of the holiday season and he could easily be coaxed into a jig or to break out his fiddle, truly a jolly old elf. We shared New Years Day dinners and none of us will ever forget my aunt's perfect Cornish game hens and my Dad asking where the turkey was after we finished them.

These are the ghosts of Christmas past, the family members that won't be making the holy pilgrimage this year, but we can invite them anyway. Simply turn out all the lights but the candles and the Christmas tree, relax in the quiet of the evening, and raise a glass in a toast and say, "Merry Christmas, welcome home."

Enjoy your Christmas and God bless us every one. At least, that's what McGregor says.

The Music of Christmas

It is with mixed feelings that we hear that vinyl phonograph records are returning. It is good news because the sound is so much better than the overly compressed music they have been producing for the past couple of decades, but on the other hand so many of us have hauled those wonderful old cabinet stereos off to the dump.

Most homes had the combination turn table, AM/FM radio receiver and maybe even an 8track player, all installed in a mahogany cabinet that took up a large portion of the living room or den. We could stack four or five LP records on the turntable and have hours of uninterrupted, commercial free music.

In our house at Christmas time, we would dig to the bottom the pile of records and bring out all the Christmas classics. We would sing along with Mitch Miller and the Gang's Christmas Favorites as we decorated the tree and everyone had a copy of the all-time best selling Merry Christmas by Bing Crosby.

We would frown when Mom would put on Mario Lanza Sings Christmas Songs or Arthur Godfrey strumming his ukulele, but we could always counter with Elvis' Christmas album as long as Dad wasn't home.

My Aunt and Uncle had the sound track to White Christmas and Bing Crosby and Danny Kaye sounded like they were right there in the room booming out of those big cabinet speakers.

Music was and is a big part of the Christmas season for many and often one song might bring back a flood of memories about a loved one, a special moment or a special place. It is good to hear that the pure sounds to go along with memories are returning.

There are lots of Christmas specials airing now, starring new singers and sometimes I have to listen to the song for a minute before I recognize it. They seem to want to change the tempo, add or subtract lyrics or make a big production out of a simple carol.

There were Christmas specials that we all had to watch. Andy Williams would bring on his brothers and the Maguire sisters or the Osmonds and an hour of pure harmony would declare that it was The Most Wonderful Time of the Year.

For Canadian content we never missed the Christmas specials of our own icons. Tommy Hunter, Canada's Country Gentleman, would sing along with the Rhythm Pals, Anita Shear and many great Canadian performers.

We surely had to be quiet when Don Messer's Jubilee presented their Christmas Special. Don Messer and His

Islanders would lead off the show with Goin to the Barn Dance Tonight then share the stage with new comers like Stompin' Tom or that young Anne Murray girl from back home in Nova Scotia.

Charlie Chamberlin would belt out Christmas in Killarney and then team up with Marg Osburne on Go Tell it on the Mountain.

There were many artists would produce a Christmas show. Liberace, Garry Moore, Rita McNeil, and Anne Murray would all have a special show and we circled those dates in our TV Guides.

I think it's great that vinyl is on the comeback, now we just have to resurrect some of the old singers to record again because they know how to put the feeling into the music. There should be a law that only Gene Autrey can sing Rudolph the Red Nose Reindeer. At least that's what McGregor says.

The Memories of Christmas

Dave made the driveway grade up to the road, shifted down and spun the old International pickup onto the hard packed snow. His grandson Donny chattered away about the tree they were going get, what he had asked Santa for and what gifts he had bought or made for everyone.

Grandpa settled the truck into the two ruts and made his way along the lane, only having to move over once to let the Simpsons by with a wave and a "Merry Christmas."

They got to the wood lot and trudged through knee deep snow until they found a clearing with the just the right tree. They laid down the burlap and the two of them dug out the root ball and tied it up. Grandpa explained that it would be planted beside the others after Christmas and they would eventually make a nice wind break along the east fence line.

As they pulled back into the yard, Dave noticed there was no visitor's car there yet. They carried in the tree and plunked in the barrel stave tub that his son Dan had retrieved from the barn. Donny opened the box of decorations and, after Mom had placed a string of lights around the branches, he began skillfully applying the old paper chains, baubles and hand carved ornaments.

Mary came out from the kitchen rubbing her hands on her apron. She gave Dave a hug and said, "I think that's the best tree we've ever had." Dave gave her a peck on the cheek and thought this wasn't the time to mention that she said that every year.

He followed her back into the kitchen where pots of vegetables, all from their own garden, bubbled and steamed on the stove top filling the kitchen with a combination of smells that only materialized at Christmas.

He made a rum and eggnog for himself and Dan and walked over to the window just as a pair of headlights swung in off the road. "I think they're here," he called into the kitchen. He went to the door and watched the big Buick Roadmaster with Alberta plates slide to a stop beside his truck.

His sister-in law gave him a hug at the doorway and headed for Mary. His brother Don grabbed two big suitcases out of the trunk and made his way to the door. He stopped at the threshold and Dave smiled and said, "Don, Don it's so good to see you after all these years."

"Dave, Dave, Dave you have to wake up and have something to eat," his care aid whispered. Dave opened his eyes and took in the stark whiteness of his small room. The Christmas smells had been replaced with an antiseptic, sterile odour. "Dave, at least have some soup, you have to keep your strength up."

Dave waved away the soup, turned on his side and pulled the covers up. He had to go back to sleep and get back to the kitchen. Mary would be asking him to take the turkey out of the oven any minute now. That was always his job.

This weekend is about making memories that you can bundle and save and hide away until you need them. Make sure they contain all the best things about the season, the smells, the sounds and the love. Merry Christmas to all, God bless us, every one. At least that's what McGregor says.

A Child's View of Christmas

Our Christmas Bureau operation has been in the rented bank building for over a month already this year. Thanks to the good folks at Coast Capital Savings we once again have a warm and dry facility to operate from. We have been registering clients, matching up sponsors, bringing in toys and donations and merrily going about the rewarding task of extending a hand to those in need.

A lady and two little girls blew in out of the wind and rain and as Mom pushed the stroller over to the registration desk, her four year daughter stood with her hands in her coat pocket and took it all in. She walked over to where we have a model Christmas train set up and I switched it on, pointing out the presents in one of the cars and the elf on the caboose.

She watched for a minute then smiled at me and said, "Well mister, you sure have a beautiful place here!"

I took a look around and realized she was right. There were sparkling snowflakes hanging from the ceiling, a lighted Christmas tree, stuffed toys of all shapes and sizes, huge candy canes and garland and some charming ladies with friendly smiles. To a four year old it wasn't a borrowed bank building at all. It must have looked a lot like Santa's Workshop.

Maybe that's the secret to managing these busy weeks we have ahead of us, we have to look at the whole season from the eyes of a four year old. Instead of stressing about shopping and spending and what to wear and who to please, all we have to do is stop once in awhile amid the lights and music, look up at the stars and say, "Hey Mister, You sure have a beautiful place here!" The secret is you have to stop.

A few nights later, I was in Fort Langley for Santa's arrival to the village. Over two hundred people gathered at the dock and awaited his arrival by lighted war canoe. Most of the crowd was excited children, and one little boy clutched an envelope with "To Santa" printed on the front. I asked if he had written the letter himself and in a big toothless grin he replied, "I am giving it to Thanta as thoon as I thee him!" He was bouncing with excitement.

We cheered Santa's arrival and followed him up the street as he shouted out Ho, Ho, Ho, and lit the big tree by the train station and then the one in front of the community hall. The kids cheered at each magical wave of his arm and then lined up to talk to him.

We all know there is much more significance to the Christmas season than Santa Clause but you must remember that excitement when you were kids and Santa came to the school concert or the mall.

Why don't you write him a letter again this year? Sit down with a pen and paper and tell him what you want for this Christmas in your family. Address the envelope to Santa Claus, North Pole, HOH OHO, and put it in the mail. Look at the season from a child's eyes again. You will be surprised how good you feel.

Then come to the Christmas parades in Aldergrove and Langley City this weekend and see what a beautiful place we have here. At least that's what McGregor says.

Jim McGregor

Christmas Parade

The lights are twinkling on the trees,
December arrives on a chilly breeze,
Toy soldiers proudly marching in,
Shouting "Let the Christmas Parade begin!"

Come down early, get a place,
To share the smile on Santa's face;
Gingerbread houses on display,
Elves and Reindeer lead the way!

Grab hot chocolate, warm your hands,
Wave candy canes to lead the bands;
See snowmen cast a wishful eye
For snowflakes tumbling from the sky!

Let's get excited, join right in,
It's time to be a kid again!
Let magic settle and surround,
It's Christmas time! Come on Downtown!

A Man's Christmas Shopping Requires Serious Planning

I was wandering aimlessly through the mall last weekend. Officially, I was Christmas shopping but a man in mall in December is much like a lost hiker on a North Shore mountain. He is not sure where he is or where he's headed and he's hoping for a helicopter to pluck him to safety.

Too often, men go Christmas shopping with no plan in mind, hoping for an epiphany in the form of a bright light shining on the perfect gift for their wives. There really is no such thing. Over the years I have purchased many different items, some were well received and some got a cool reception.

Men misinterpret signals. If she says, "The toaster is on its last legs," that doesn't mean she wants a toaster for Christmas. Chances are you will buy a white one when all the rest of the appliances are stainless steel. Small appliances are not good Christmas gifts.

Clothes can be acceptable but, if you are going to peek at a pair of slacks in the closet to get the right size, make sure you choose the ones she is wearing after she lost ten pounds. Negligee can be tricky. I have learned there is a big difference between flimsy and sexy or comfortable and functional. It is too easy to send the wrong message with black lace.

Maybe tickets to a play or to an upcoming performance is a good idea. Just a reminder, the Winnipeg Ballet is a better choice than the Winnipeg Jets. A day at a spa or even a weekend getaway can be a great idea but you need to do careful planning.

One year, I arranged a weekend for two at the Harrison Hot Springs Hotel. I had the weekend package wrapped under the tree. I had pre-arranged that Grandma would take the kids for the weekend. All the way up on Friday, the conversation was light and cheerful.

When we pulled up to the hotel there was a huge banner, "Welcome to the B.C Firefighters Provincial Curling Bonspiel." It turned out that I knew over half of the men staying at the hotel, without their wives.

Our reserved table for two in the dining room became a table for six as the Surrey team joined us with funny stories and revelry. Our quiet time in the hot tub was disturbed by six burley Okanagan curlers entertaining us with witty songs and jokes. We had knocks on our room door after midnight inviting us to parties. The drive home Sunday afternoon was quiet and subdued.

I thought I had purchased the perfect gift but by not asking if there was something going on at the Hotel that weekend, I had blown it. Do the research.

A couple had become separated in the mall. She phoned him to see where he was. He answered, "Honey you know that jewellery store we were in last year and saw that diamond pendant and earrings that we thought we could maybe afford another year?"

"Yes!" she shouted excitedly.

"Well" he replied, "I'm in the pub across from that jewellery store."

I usually try to finish my column with a solution to a problem. On this topic, men, you are on your own.

Like the North Shore hiker, before you enter the mall plan your day, know where the pitfalls are and be prepared to spend the night. At Least that's what McGregor says.

Memories in the Christmas Baking

I have a cup of coffee and a slice of eggnog bread sitting beside my laptop for inspiration. I purchased the loaf of eggnog bread at a church bazaar mostly because I had never tasted any before and the ingredients in the recipe attached were mostly things I'm not supposed to eat. It sounded delicious and weighed about five pounds so I was pretty sure it had to be good.

Everyone should visit at least one church bazaar prior to the holidays. Each one of them offers a bake sale and the delicacies come from someone's kitchen, individually baked and not mass-produced in a commercial bakery.

Most of the items spread out on the long tables are lovingly concocted from recipes that have been handed down from generations and maybe only come to light at this time of year. Everyone has his or her favorite Christmas treats. Maybe its Uncle Duncan's squares or Aunty Marg's cookies or grandma's Christmas pudding.

I can remember the yellowed pieces of paper or little cards that appeared on Mom's counter at Christmas time, each one with faded writing describing the ingredients and baking instructions. Nothing was stored in a computer file and no one Googled a recipe. Those hieroglyphics were folded in the pages of cookbooks or tucked at the back of the kitchen drawer.

I recall one day when we were setting up a book section for a garage sale and one of helpers tossed an old cookbook into the discard pile. "It's all stained and scribbled in, "she said. I picked it up and I was immediately transported into a warm country kitchen.

The stains were from drops of jam that had dripped from a tasting spoon, or from sauces that were being transferred from the pan to the pudding. The cook book had been well used by a serious cook.

The scribbles were extra instructions about oven temperatures or to add cream instead of milk or a note that the recipe ingredients didn't make as many cookies as the book said it would. In the margin on one cookie page the note says, "These are Gary's favorite." So we can only assume that any time Gary came for a visit, those cookies were on the plate by his coffee. I threw a toonie in the box and bought that book. It seemed just too much of a treasure to throw in a dumpster.

We all have a special recipe for our Christmas. The concerts we go to, the type and size of tree we get, who we send cards to, who we phone, when we decorate and how much we spend. We know when to mix in other people and who we can blend in with whom.

Some people are always a bit too sweet and others too sour. Some are tasteful and others leave a bad taste in our mouth. The trick is not to have too much of either one.

We all remember that perfect Christmas and how great everyone felt and it seems we try to recreate it every year. But, unlike the enduring, faded notes in those old cookbooks, the ingredients of our Christmas' change from year to year. Some old ones are not there anymore and it seems new ones are always being added.

Just keep it all at an even temperature and don't let it boil over. At least that's what McGregor says.

Recipe for a Great Christmas Morning

Ingredients
Snow
Laughter
Fireplace
Ribbons and Bows
Children
Memories

Add a cup of crisp sunshine
Precisely at dawn;
Spread snow, thick like sugar
Across the front lawn.

Blend in a Yule log
With it's soft pleasant glow,
Pouring flickers and shadows
On each ribbon and bow.

Shake in some giggles
As the children awake;
Dissolve last year's problems
In new memories you make.

Combine family together,
Sprinkle good will their way
Stir it well, serve up Christmas
In the old fashioned way!

Recipe for a Happy Family Christmas Dinner

1 cup friendly words
Pinch of warm personality
2 heaping cups of understanding
Dash of humour
4 heaping tsp. time and patience

Measure words carefully. Add heaping cups of understanding. Use generous amounts of time and patience. Cook on front burners, but keep temperature low; do not boil! Add generous amounts of humour and a pinch of warm personality. Season to taste with spice of life. Serve in individual molds.

Boxing Day Leftovers

The first year we were married my wife boldly offered to have everyone over for Christmas dinner. She was a great cook and we loved to entertain so I agreed and we worked together to plan the menu and mix the two family traditions as best we could.

We knew we had to have turkey and ham to keep both fathers happy and certain vegetables had to be cooked a certain way and the dessert had to have both Canadian and Dutch flavours. We started early the day before to prepare and we discussed who should sit where.

We discussed how to defuse potential situations and we arranged for pre-dinner snacks and made sure we had beer, rum, eggnog and Akavit, a nasty Dutch schnapps that sneaks up on you and makes you say things you wouldn't normally say.

The evening went great and the meal was well received by all. For dessert you had a choice of traditional hot Christmas pudding with hard sauce, apple pie or slices of thick moist Christmas cake. We all ate too much. The rest of the evening passed with games and conversations and when it was time to leave my wife packed up turkey for everyone to take home and we turned out the lights, congratulated each other and went to bed.

Boxing Day morning arrived and I slipped quietly out of bed, I turned on the TV and found a football game on and went into the kitchen to make a pot of coffee. The house was quiet, the neighbourhood was quiet and I didn't have to work. The plan was to just sit and relax after yesterday's planning and presentation of dinner.

After a bit I decided to make something to eat. Not just anything, that perfect Boxing Day clubhouse sandwich. Even while I was eating Christmas dinner I was tasting that sandwich. Thick slices of turkey and ham, stuffing, cranberry sauce, two big slices of dill pickle, mayo, salt and pepper and washed down with a glass of eggnog.

I opened the fridge door and started moving things around and I couldn't find the turkey or ham. Where were the leftovers? With trepidation, I opened the freezer compartment and there was my sandwich. All the ingredients neatly packed into Tupperware containers or Ziplock bags, labelled with the date on them, frozen solid.

They say we never truly know our spouses when we first get married. How was I to know that a promise not to freeze Christmas leftovers should have been included in our wedding vows?

On closer examination the news got worse. Scraping the frost off the containers I could see the word "soup" written on a couple. When I opened them there were no big, thick slices, just diced up chunks.

Where was the drumstick? Where was my Boxing Day sandwich? Sure, I could have put it in the microwave but it's just not the same. It has to be carved right off the carcass and layered neatly on the bread. You can't place little chunks on the slice of bread like a jigsaw puzzle.

But we were still newlyweds and when she got up and offered to make bacon and eggs, I said that would be just fine. But I could see Uncle Bob at home biting into my Boxing Day clubhouse. There is nothing like Christmas dinner leftovers, guard them with your life. At least that's what McGregor says.

Christmas is in the Silence

Christmas Eve is my favorite time of the Christmas season. Finally, the peace and quiet that is supposed to be associated with this time of year has settled, all is calm, all is bright.

If you haven't bought all the gifts you planned to, you're pretty much out of luck unless they still sell it at 7-11. Most of the stores close early as the shoppers rush home with their presents and if you forgot the scotch tape or wrapping paper, it's time to get creative. I once wrapped a Christmas gift in Happy Birthday paper, trying to convince the recipient that it was a very important birthday after all, but they didn't buy it.

The traffic is almost non-existent. Everyone has made it home because Christmas Eve is all about being home, being with family and only a few people are out and about doing some last minute visiting or maybe heading to a church service. There are no long lineups at the intersections but strings of streetlights, even stop lights, still blink a bright red and green.

I recall the quiet of our house when I was a boy. After dinner, we maybe went to our rooms to do the final gift wrapping and then sneak them down under the tree so brothers and sisters couldn't guess what we had bought.

The TV was off and Bing Crosby and Frank Sinatra Christmas records were dug out from their hiding place in the old hassock and spun out carols from the record player. Usually a board game or a deck of cards appeared and we sat around the kitchen table until it was time to wake up Dad if we had decided to go to the Christmas Eve church service. People laughing, people passing, dressed in holiday style.

Some years, my older brothers and sisters would go to midnight mass with some of their Catholic friends and I was jealous that they got to stay up so late but we usually had a party of own.

Mom would make some hot cocoa, but not with hot water and mix out of a can. Milk would be heated to boiling in a pan on the stove and then cocoa added and stirred to a froth. No other hot chocolate has ever tasted like that. Popcorn was the preferred snack and again, no hot air machines or microwave envelopes.

The stove was still hot so a little cooking oil was poured in the pan then the popcorn kernels were added. Shaking the pan over the stove was an older brother job and soon the popcorn was pinging against the lid and when the lid was removed, popcorn cascaded over the edge of the pan. Children laughing, in the air there's a feeling of Christmas.

At bedtime there were still no presents from Santa but the rule was, if you stopped believing in Santa, there was no gift from him for you under the tree. So carefully the cookies and milk were set out and we were sent to bed. Our day was over. This was Santa's big scene, soon it would be Christmas day.

The magic is in the silence. Later, as a father and after Santa had laid out his gifts, eaten the cookies and drank the milk, that silence reminded me what all this noisy celebration was about.

And above all this bustle you'll hear, silver bells. At least that's what McGregor says

Hot Chocolate

It was a perfect evening for a Christmas Parade, crisp and clear and cold enough to want a hot chocolate. That was good because the Christmas Bureau folks were providing hot chocolate by donation outside our Fraser Highway office and the crowds were gathering early.

Kelly the Coffee Guy from Crown Coffee supplied the hot chocolate and thermos dispensers, a couple of husbands that are used to being in hot water were in charge of kettles and urns, Barry played carols on the electric organ to attract the crowds and the tireless Christmas Bureau volunteers kept the cups full and passed them out to the waiting gloved hands.

It was fun to watch the families as they spied the hot chocolate stand. Most were hustling along the street in search of their perfect parade viewing spot but when they spotted us they would detour with kids in tow and leave clutching a steaming cup of the warm, brown libation. After all, it is the perfect family drink and you don't have to worry about how many you have or when you have them.

Dad is not going to be stopped in a roadblock to be confronted by a policeman saying, "Sir, your entire family has brown moustaches, you're going to have to blow into the Chocalizer." Come to think of it, no one would probably pass a "Chocalizer" test for the next three weeks.

As one woman walked away sipping from her cup I heard her say, "Mmmm, this is good, it reminds me of ice skating back home in Alberta." That conjured up some memories for me. We didn't have the opportunity to ice skate outdoors much here in the Lower Mainland, but once in awhile the flats at Fry's Corner, 176th and Fraser Highway, would flood and then freeze over creating a 10-acre skating rink.

Families would gather, impromptu hockey games would break out, figure skaters would practice pirouettes among the tufts of grass, but most would just skate. My B.C. brothers and I would slip and stumble and fall but my Saskatchewan parents would put their arms around each other's waists, hold hands and skate smoothly out of sight in the perfect rhythm they had learned on those far away rivers and ponds.

Once we got home, Mom would boil a big pan of milk and take down the yellow can of Cocoa from the cupboard and soon we would all be sipping the magic elixir that would bring circulation back to our toes and warm our souls from the inside out.

Hot water and chocolate mix are you really need but you can get this winter drink in many forms. Coffee shops can make you $5.00 cup with whipped cream and maybe a design floating on top. You can add mint or sprinkle a touch of nutmeg or add a cinnamon stick or a couple of marshmallows. You can take it in a to go cup on your walk or have in a big mug and sip it while you read or relax, a great break on that Christmas shopping survivor episode at the mall, or you can drink it just before bed and it won't keep you awake.

If you want to be more adventurous, Google hot chocolate and you'll find recipes from around the world. In the end we raised enough to sponsor a family, and that warms the soul too. At least that's what McGregor says.

Enduring Board Games

One of the many good things about the Christmas season is getting together with family. Well, I suppose that depends on the family and some of you may be glad they've packed up and headed home already.

Sitting around and talking all at once seems to be a great pastime in my family, It is somewhat like you see on those glimpses into the New York Stock Exchange and when your turn comes to speak, you have to be quick and make sure you've been listening to all five conversations.

One of the discussions turned to playing board games and how many of the old games are making a comeback and people are turning off the electronics and sitting around the kitchen table again.

We always had plenty of games and we played a lot. In those days they advertised them as "entertaining and educational," and we certainly got an education.

For instance Monopoly was a popular game with us kids. It was amazing how fifteen minutes into the game, good Christian, rural children had changed. Suddenly we were slumlords buying up low rent houses on Marvin Gardens, Virginia, and Atlantic Avenues. We roared with laughter when one of our siblings had to go to jail and we hoarded cash every time we passed go.

Soon we strived to be elitist developers and laughed diabolically if one of our poorer lot landed on our newly upgraded Park Place or Boardwalk and yet little did we know that the educational component was supposed to inform us that someday Park Place would be a lot in Brookswood and the banker would be even more difficult to deal with than our big sister was during the game.

The Monopoly game has had quite a history since it appeared in 1934 and has gone through a lot of changes. In 1941 the British Secret Service had special games made up that included hollowed out pieces that contained maps or messages and real cash and had them distributed by fake charities to prisoner of war camps in Germany.

Some modern versions have done away with the cash and have an electronic feature that uses debit or credit cards. The property prices in the new games have increased from $200.00 to $2,000,000.00 and the penalties now include Visa interest. Talk about educational!

No doubt a Langley version would have you constructing an overpass on the Pennsylvania Railroad to make it easier to get from St. James Place to Virginia Ave, the money coming from Community Chest of course.

One year we got a large crokinole board that had the crokinole game on one side and checkers, chess and a marble board game on the back. We had that for years and I have no idea what became o f it.

Speaking of mysteries, Clue was always a favourite and taught us to have secrets and to accuse each other of terrible crimes. "Aha, it was you Colonel Mustard, in the conservatory, with the lead pipe!" I'm sure in today's Clue game Col. Mustard's lawyer would have him free in twenty-four hours.

But the concept of a family sitting around a kitchen table together was one of the values people like Hasbro or Parker Brothers was trying to promote, and it is nice to see it's making a return.

We may just be a roll of the dice away from talking to each other again. At least that's what McGregor says.

Un-Decorating

What do the Rolling Stones and Christmas trees have in common? After you've dragged one out of your living room, there will be needles all over the floor.

That's an old joke but I'm having an end of the year clearance and everything must go. This is the weekend to un-decorate, put last year back in the boxes and tuck it away in the attic or the crawl space.

Some people tell me that they had "had enough" last weekend and cleaned up then. Other traditionalists wait until Twelfth Night, January 6th, before they pull down the mistletoe and drag out the tree. For most of us though, as soon as we put up that new calendar and see January 1st, out comes the vacuum cleaner and away goes Christmas past. There is always a sense of completion when the house is back to normal, the rooms look bigger and brighter and we have an optimistic glow about the upcoming year.

We had a nice tree this year, when we got him his name tag said, "Douglas Fir". Now I had never thought of giving a tree a name but we brought Douglas home with us and he was great house guest. He never ate anything, drank a little each day, looked great in a skirt and was there to welcome me in the morning and say goodnight when I turned out the lights. You may be concerned that I'm talking to trees but there is just my teen-aged son and I here and a conversation with a six-foot fir tree elicits pretty much the same response as a conversation with a six-foot teenaged boy. I felt bad about leaving Douglas in the school parking lot but he looked pretty "chipper" when I drove away.

There is a marked difference in un-decorating the interior of your home, which can be done anytime, or taking down the exterior decorations, which any man will tell you, "has to wait until the right day." You can't take down outside lights while College bowl games, Junior Hockey tournaments or NFL Payoffs are in progress. If the weather is bad, even a major billiard tournament or International Poker Challenge will take precedence as well.

I received a call one January day on my Fire Department radio that a woman was stranded on her roof. I was only a block away so I responded to find her ladder had slipped while she had been taking down the Christmas lights. I told her to sit tight until the truck came. She didn't want another truck, just me to put the ladder back. I didn't think this was the time to discuss four man ladder protocols or the Management's role in the collective agreement so I convinced her it would be safer to wait.

During our conversation, it came out that yesterday was "a good day to take down the lights but he had sat on his butt watching the Super Bowl." I felt bad for him, driving home expecting roast beef and mashed potatoes but getting cold shoulder and hot tongue instead. During the Super Bowl is never the right day.

Good luck with your un-decorating and no matter how good a job you do, you'll find a stray shepherd, angel or Santa a week later and your lights will be a big tangled mess next December, at least that's what McGregor says.

ALSO BY JIM MCGREGOR:

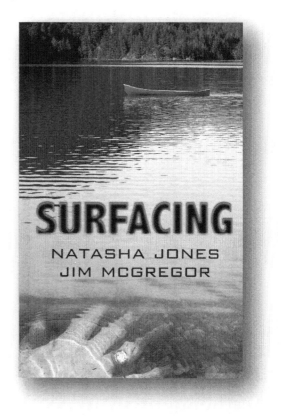

Available in print and e-book.

82408632R00129

Made in the USA
Columbia, SC
16 December 2017